Sebastian's Arrows

Letters and Mementos
of Salvador Dalí
and Federico García Lorca

Sebastian's Arrows

Letters and Mementos of Salvador Dalí and Federico García Lorca

Edited, translated annotated, and with a prologue
by Christopher Maurer

SWAN ISLE PRESS
CHICAGO

Swan Isle Press, Chicago 60640-8790

Printed in the United States of America
First Edition

Acknowledgments are made to Fundació Gala-Salvador Dalí and Fundación Federico García Lorca for their support and generous respective grants of permission to use texts and images; © Salvador Dalí, Gala-Salvador Dalí/Artists Rights Society (ARS) New York, all rights reserved, permission for "Collage de los Zapatos" and "El Casamiento de Buster Keaton;" Enrique Sabater, permission to reprint excerpt from *My Secret Life* by Salvador Dalí, ©2004 by DASA Editions, N.V., all rights reserved; Museo Nacional de Escultura for permission to include *San Sebastian* by Alonso Berruguete© Museo Nacional de Escultura, Valladolid, Spain; The Program for Cultural Cooperation between Spain's Ministry of Education, Culture and Sports and United States Universities; and the Illinois Arts Council, a State of Illinois agency

"Imagination Inspiration, Evasion," by Federico García Lorca, reconstructed and translated by Christopher Maurer, published in *jubilat*, issue 7, 2003; and *Harper's Magazine*, vol. 309, no. 1852, 2004. Letters 23 and 25 published in *Northwest Review*, 30:1, 1992.

Library of Congress Cataloging-in-Publication Data
Dalí, Salvador, 1904-
Sebastian's Arrows: Letters and Mementos of Salvador Dalí and Federico García Lorca / edited, translated, annotated, and with a prologue by Christopher Maurer.
p. cm.
Includes bibliographical references and index.
ISBN 0-9678808-8-2 (alk. paper)
1. Dalí, Salvador, 1904- —Correspondence. 2. García Lorca, Federico, 1898-1936—Correspondence. 3. Artists—Spain—Correspondence. 4. Authors, Spanish—20th century—Correspondence. 5. Dalí, Salvador, 1904- —Friends and associates. 6. García Lorca, Federico, 1898-1936—Friends and associates. 7. Arts, Spanish—20th century. 8. Aesthetics, Modern—20th century. I. García Lorca, Federico, 1898-1936. II. Maurer, Christopher. III. Title.
ND813.D3A3 2004
709'.2—dc22
[B] 2004058128

This book has been made possible in part by generous grants of permission from:

FUNDACIÓ GALA-SALVADOR DALÍ

The Gala-Salvador Dalí Foundation. The Gala-Salvador Dalí Foundation was created in 1983 at the express desire of Salvador Dalí (1904-1989) with the aim of promoting, administering, conserving, and protecting the work and artistic legacy of the painter. (www.salvador-dalí.org)

Fundación Federico García Lorca

The Federico García Lorca Foundation. The fundamental purpose of the Federico García Lorca Foundation is to promote the study and diffusion not only of the Spanish poet's own work, but also of the numerous artistic endeavors which influenced or were influenced by the poet and his work. (www.garcia-lorca.org)

Swan Isle Press gratefully acknowledges the generous grant of subvention by Spain's Ministry of Education, Culture and Sports, and United States Universities in support of the publication of this book as part of Spain's Program for Cultural Cooperation.

Illinois ARTS Council

Swan Isle Press is funded in part by a generous grant from the Illinois Arts Council, A State of Illinois Agency.

www.swanislepress.com

To Chata

Contents

Acknowledgments

"I've spent the entire Sunday afternoon rereading all of your letters," Dalí writes to Lorca in 1926. "My dear, they are extraordinary! Every line suggests numerous books, plays, paintings, etc. etc. etc." One of the tragic aspects of their friendship is that most of García Lorca's letters to Dalí have been lost, removed perhaps from the painter's residence in Port Lligat in 1982 (described in Gibson, *Shameful Life*, 651). Fortunately, the poet's letters to Dalí's sister Anna María survive, and are given here both because of their intrinsic beauty and because they cast light on the poet's work and on his relationship with Dalí. For the Spanish text of Lorca's letters, I have followed *Epistolario completo*, and for those of Dalí, the edition of Rafael Santos Torroella, *Salvador Dalí escribe a Federico García Lorca*, which contains facsimiles of many of the texts and their accompanying drawings and collages. Lorca's lecture, "Sketch of the New Painting," is presented in English for the first time, as are the complete versions of many of the letters included here. Lorca's lecture, "Imagination, Inspiration, Evasion," has never before been published in book form.

The original manuscripts of Dalí's letters to Lorca are in the Fundación Federico García Lorca, Madrid, and those of Lorca to Dalí are in the Fundació Gala-Salvador Dalí and in private collections (for detailed information, see *EC*). The editor and publisher are grateful for the respective grants of permission from the Fundació Gala-Salvador Dalí, Figueres, and Fundación Federico García Lorca, Madrid, without whose support this book would not have been possible. We are deeply grateful to the Program for Cultural Cooperation Between Spain's Ministry of Education, Culture and Sports, and U.S. Universities for its generous grant of subvention toward publication; and to the Illinois Arts Council, a State of Illinois Agency, for its generous support. I wish to extend my deep gratitude as well to a number of individuals including Manuel Fernández-Montesinos García, William P. Kosmas, Joan Manuel Sevillano Campalans, Montse Aguer, Jordi Falgàs, Enrique Sabater, Antonio Ramos Gascón, Holly Zimmerman-LeVoir; and special thanks to Andrew A. Anderson, the first editor of some of these texts, who provided helpful comments on the prologue. The translation of "Imagination, Inspiration, Evasion" first appeared in *jubilat*, 7 (2003); and was also reprinted in *Harper's Magazine*, (September, 2004). Letters 23 and 24 were first published in *Northwest Review*, 30:1 (1992).

Prologue

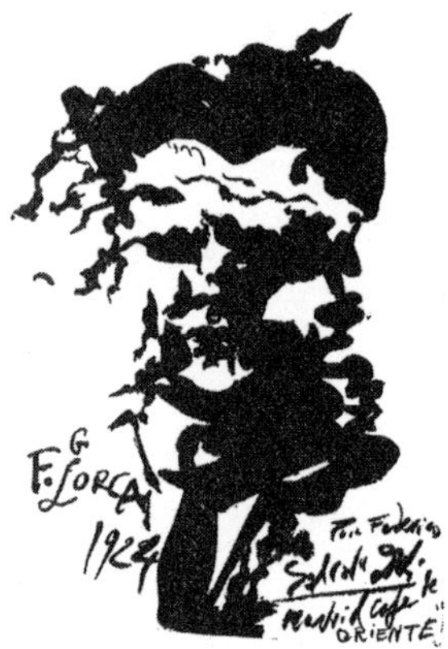

Salvador Dalí, portrait of Federico García Lorca, pen and ink, dated and signed: "F. G. Lorca 1924. Para Federico Salvador Dalí. Madrid, Café de Oriente." Dimensions and location unknown; first published in *The Secret Life of Salvador Dalí* (203), where the painter writes: "The shadow of Maldoror hovered over my life, and it was just at this period that for the duration of an eclipse precisely another shadow, that of Federico García Lorca, came and darkened the virginal originality of my spirit and of my flesh. // During this time I knew several elegant women on whom my hateful cynicism desperately grazed for moral and erotic fodder. I avoided Lorca and the group, which grew to be his group more and more. This was the culminating moment of his irresistible personal influence—and the only moment of my life when I thought I glimpsed the torture that jealousy can be. Sometimes we would be walking, the whole group of us, along El Paseo de la Castellana on our way to the café where we held our usual literary meetings and where I knew Lorca would shine like a mad and fiery diamond. Suddenly I would set off at a run, and no one would see me for three days... No one has ever been able to tear from me the secret of these flights, and I don't intend to unveil it now—at least not yet..."

Sea sirens on bicycles of coral, stray breasts and liberated fingers. Grapes pursuing a fish and "beastlings" that crumble like peanuts in the hand. Arrows of St. Sebastian. Motifs of a legendary friendship, that of Salvador Dalí (1904-1989) and Federico García Lorca (1898-1936).

The two of them met in early 1923, in the Residencia de Estudiantes, Madrid, a residential college intended to provide ideal conditions of study for a couple of hundred young men judged to be among the future leaders of Spanish society. Dalí was a timid eighteen-year-old enrolled at the Special School of Drawing at the Academy of San Fernando. The ebullient Lorca, six years older, had come to Madrid in 1919, interrupting his studies at the University of Granada and promising his parents and friends that he would publish his poems, stage his plays, and learn, somehow, to make a living as a writer. Their daily comraderie at the "Resi"—and in Toledo with Luis Buñuel and others—came to a halt when Dalí was expelled from the Academy, declaring that his professors were not qualified to examine him (Gibson, *Shameful Life*, 182), but the friendship survived thanks to visits and letters. During Easter Week 1925 Lorca visited Dalí on the Costa Brava: his first trip ever to

Catalonia. In Barcelona, in June 1927, Dalí designed the stage settings for one of Lorca's plays, *Mariana Pineda*, and arranged for an exhibit of the poet's drawings at a prestigious gallery. By the time of their estrangement in 1928, after Dalí wrote Lorca a long, sharply critical letter about *The Gypsy Ballads*, the world of each had been deeply altered. Dalí focussed his attention on Surrealism, collaborated with Buñuel on two avant-garde films (*Un Chien Andalou* and *L'Age d'Or*), and began to paint in the radically different manner that would lead to the "paranoiac critical method" for which he is best known. Lorca plunged into the "streets and dreams" of New York, in search of a poetics that could accommodate the loneliness and alienation of modern urban civilization. It was, Dalí once remarked, a "tragic, passionate" relationship. Except for a brief meeting in 1935, the two never spoke again.

In the letters, lectures and mementos gathered here, two poetic worlds come so intimately into contact that critics sometimes refer to an "época lorquiana" in the work of Dalí, and an "época daliniana" in that of García Lorca (Santos Torroella 1984; Hernández 1989). In retrospect, their aesthetics seem very different. Like any lyric poet, Lorca was in love with the accidents of time, and his poetics had always been grounded in tradition. For several years before he met Dalí, he had believed that poetry was as much an anonymous, oral phenomenon—rooted in "popular" art transmitted from parents to their children—as it was the creation of learned, individual poets. One did not merely "write" poetry; one heard it and sang it. The narrative mysteries of the ballad and traditional song, the searing lyrics of *cante jondo*, mattered as much to him as the stately syntax of Luis de Góngora or the cordial prose of Cervantes; and he felt most strongly attracted to those learned artists—Gustavo Adolfo Bécquer, Antonio Machado, Manuel de Falla—who drew most deeply and gracefully on the traditional lyric. For Lorca, "tradition" was not a matter of archaeology, social pretension, or antiquarianism (the point wasn't to *collect* ballads or popular stories)—it lay around him in the historical "palimpsest" of his native Granada: a record in plaster, stone and parchment of the co-existence of Romans and Jews, Muslims and Christians. Traditional "songs and sweets"—lullabies, the cries of street vendors, ballads, popular cuisine—brought the past to one's senses better than architecture and literature, making it "live and quivering as a frog" (Lorca *DS* 8). And yet, if the tradition of Granada was a source of inspiration, it also carried its burden of "historical melancholy." In Granada he felt the "void of something that has forever ended." Dalí—and through him, Barcelona and Catalonia—offered Lorca his first encounter with Spanish modernity, an aesthetic atmosphere where the "modern"—not only the city and region, but also their social customs—seemed to harmonize in its simplicity with the "classical" (there was an ancient Greek and Roman colony at Empuries, and Catalonia was filled with ancient ruins). Whether in the fishing town of Cadaqués (where the Dalí family had its summer residence), in Figueres (their permanent home), or in Barcelona, a cosmopolitan "Mediterranean" culture offered a world more open, less encumbered by the past, than either Granada (with its enclosed spaces and Muslim arabesques) or the relative cultural isolation of the Castilian heartland. No doubt the Residencia de Estudiantes provided a stimulating intellectual atmosphere, but both painter and poet were probably aware that it was the "periphery," the provinces, that would enliven Spanish culture. "*¡Basta ya de Castilla!*"—Enough of Castile!—Lorca had written to a friend in 1923, announcing a book of Andalusian ballads, and the friend—the critic Melchor Fernández Almagro—had assented, condemning Castilian thought for its "vulgarity, garbanzo-bean mentality, dust and adobe, teacher-training courses and continuing education."

> Here [in Madrid] the problem isn't to train but to create, to construct something! How lovely it would be if broken-down, sordid Castile would let itself be absorbed by men of the North—who would give it strength and covetousness—and by the men of the South, who would give it grace and tenderness and an aptitude for daydream. (*EC* 148)

In Catalonia, that "creation" and "construction" seemed ubiquitous, and to Lorca "the group of intellectuals in Barcelona" seemed "one of the best in Europe" (*EC* 266). "Barcelona is very different, isn't it?" he wrote wrote excitedly after his first visit to Dalí and his family.

> There one finds the Mediterranean, the spirit, the adventure, the elevated dream of perfect love. There are palms, people from every country, surprising advertisements, gothic towers and the rich urban high tide created by typewriters. How I enjoy being there, with that air and that passion [...] I, who am a ferocious Catalanist, identified greatly with those people, so fed up with Castile and so creative. *(Selected Letters*, 69)

It was Dalí who drew Lorca, more forcefully than anyone, toward what the painter called the "eurhythmia" of contemporary civilization: photography and the cinema, dance, sport, the perspectives of contemporary science. In a "manifesto" of 1927, Dalí casts an admiring eye over all that modernity has to offer:

THERE IS	the cinema
THERE ARE	stadia, boxing, rugby, tennis, and a thousand other sports.
THERE IS	the popular music of today: jazz and modern dance
THERE ARE	motor and aeronautics shows
THERE ARE	beach games
THERE ARE	beauty competitions in the open air
THERE IS	the fashion show
THERE IS	the naked performer under the electric lights of the music hall
THERE IS	modern music.

(Raeburn. *EY*, 221)

And so on, through ocean liners and the gramophone, contemporary architecture and literature; "encyclopedias of extraordinary erudition," and—more mysteriously—"an immobile ear over a small puff of smoke." The "tradition" Dalí invoked, when he invoked it at all, was the drawing of Raphael or Ingres or the careful brushwork of Vermeer. For him, tradition was the product of intelligence and patient technique, not of a rustic "popular" muse, and it led to "clarity," not to the "mystery" Lorca held out as a necessary condition of art. "¡No hay claridad!"—there is no clarity!—the poet heard him say, again and again. For Lorca, who followed in the steps of Antonio Machado and Juan Ramón Jiménez, what had always mattered were the narrative gaps or "lacunae" of a ballad—the part of the story that disappeared with the passage of time. The traditional poetry he emulated in his own work was a collective art of narrative fragments, a verbal and musical ruin shrouded with mystery and emotion. For Dalí, *all* ruins were uncleanly, any display of emotion—in literature or in life—made him uneasy, and "anecdote" of any sort was anathema: neither a painting nor a poem should "tell" anything at all. In his thought of the mid 1920s "emotion," "pathos," and anecdote led straight to the vulgar sentimentality he called "putrefaction" (he begged Lorca to collaborate with him on a satirical book, *Los putrefactos*) and neither romantic love nor anything that looked like "inner life" was welcome in his world. An "asepsia," an "irony," a strict "hygiene" of the emotions went hand-in-glove with the physical hygiene he insisted on and associated with modernity: showers, boxing, exercise, shaving, abstemiousness appear in his writing as antidotes to Bohemianism, romanticism, and wine-soaked notions of Art. *Anti*-Art was what brought a smile to his face, and at the movies it was stone-faced Buster Keaton or the irony of Harry Langdon that attracted him, not the soulful eyes of Lorca's beloved Charlie Chaplin, for it was Keaton and Langdon who skidded over the surface of things, and Dalí wanted to believe that only the epidermis mattered—that the surface was *all there was*: there were no "inner depths." When Lorca talked to him, at the Residencia, about "the life of the spirit," Dalí heard only blather. "His fantasy reaches as far as his hands," Lorca wrote in his "Ode to Salvador Dalí," and Dalí must have taken it as a compliment. "[For me] the inside of things is still a superficial reality," he wrote to a friend in 1927. "What is deep is still an epidermis... Things *have no other meaning besides their strict objectivity;* and to me this accounts for their miraculous poetry [...] I don't see any question to answer in the world which *surrounds* us; I only see objectivities to register" (Monegal 152). *Santa Objetividad*—Blessed Objectivity—was a saint he often invoked (Hernández 1997).

The determination to stay "on the surface of things"—within the domain of sight—is apparent in early paintings like *Basket of Bread* (1926), the portrait of his father (1925), and in the numerous sketches and oil paintings of Anna María. In his "Ode to Salvador Dalí" (1926)—an imaginative leap into another artistic universe, inspired in part by Jean Cocteau's "Ode to Picasso"—Lorca evokes a place where waves can be counted, night is reduced to "a black statue of prudence," and sirens offer not the mystery of the deep but a glass of fresh water. The stars—Romantic symbol of infinity—"have come to reveal the perfect scheme of their orbit," there is "no room" for the "inexact flora" of dream, and the flag, shorn of its patriotic symbolism, is "a simple joke." Nature and emotion are fully under control. The contrast between staying on "the surface of things" and plunging beneath the surface into "dark physiologies of the body, the central fire, the funnels of night," is fully developed in a narration—for some, a "prose poem" (Anderson 2004)—by Lorca, written in 1927, titled "St. Lucy and St. Lazarus" (127-136) where the 29-year-old poet seems to describe two distinct possibilities for the artist. The first, that of St. Lucy, which favors "the exterior of things, the clean airy beauty of the skin, the charm of slender surfaces," would appear to represent the art of Dalí in the mid-1920s. The second, that of St. Lazarus—whom Christ resurrected from the dead—probably symbolized Lorca's own poetics; although by then—1927—Lorca was beginning to see these two poles—surface and depths, clarity and mystery—as dialectical principles that are somehow reconciled in any successful work of art and, perhaps, had to be reconciled in his own relationship with Dalí. A similar antithesis occurs later in a lecture entitled "Imagination, Inspiration, Evasion" (153-162), where the poet who depends merely upon visual reality feels "sadly defrauded in his inner world," and in "Sketch of the New Painting" (167-179), where the cold mathematics of Cubism yields to an art—that of Joan Miró—governed by dream and inspiration. In both those lectures it is evident that Lorca is dealing with the challenge and provocation of Dalí's thought and work, and sometimes even echoing his language (Hernández 1989; Anderson 1991, 2004). But by then, the friendship was clearly coming to an end. Dalí approved of St. Sebastian (with his passivity, patience, and elegance) and of St. Lucy, but St. Lazarus was "the quintessence of putrefaction" (Gaillemen 114). Lorca's "Sketch of the New Painting" devotes only a single sentence to Dalí. It is two of Dalí's masters, Joan Miró and Juan Gris, who awaken Lorca's enthusiasm.

In canvases like *Honey is Sweeter than Blood, Little Cinders*, or *Apparatus and Hand* (all 1927), which Lorca had admired intensely, Dalí was pushing his "objectivity" to new extremes, vowing to dissociate objects from their customary symbolic values and reduce them to their component elements until those elements no longer "composed" anything at all and took off on their own, casting their shadows in unexpected directions, as they did in the work of Chirico or Miró.

> The minute-hands of a clock (never mind my examples, I'm not exactly looking for poetic ones) begin to have real value at the moment they stop pointing out the hours and, losing their circular rhythm and the arbitrary role our intelligence has subjected them to (pointing out the hours), they evade the clock entirely and occupy the place that would correspond to the sex organs of little bread crumbs. (letter 36,102)

One "object" which, according to a number of critics, appears frequently in Dalí's paintings and drawings of 1927-28 is the head of García Lorca, severed from its body (as in *Honey...* or *Little Cinders*) or superimposed, like an eclipse, upon—or behind—that of the painter: *Head (Draft of a Double Image)*, an unsettling sign of the fusion of two antagonistic poetic worlds. "For the duration of an eclipse," Dalí wrote many years later, the shadow of Lorca "came and darkened the virginal originality of my spirit and of my flesh."

So thoroughly did Lorca assimilate Dalí's thought on "objectivity" that he penned an imaginary dialogue between himself and Dalí. In "Corazón bleu y Coeur azul"—begun in 1927 or 1928 but never finished—the

"POET," presumably Lorca, takes pride in his metaphorical prowess—in his ability to relate any object to any other, no matter how distant, and to find an underlying "unity" in the world: thanks to the web of metaphor, all things are interconnected. The "FRIEND," probably Dalí, argues for granting objects a life of their own, and for freeing them from the bonds of metaphor and, hence, of the processes of analogy that bring them together.

> POET: It's not when I go up and down the stairs that I remember the elevator. I remember the elevator when I'm in the desert or sitting at a café table. To join a common, distant thing with the little dove that is pulsing in my fingers I need to launch my 50,000 pairs of eyes, my violet grade school [?] into the badly tempered air. After a while, thanks to them, I see the fragile thread that joins all things to each particular thing, and each thing to all.
>
> MY FRIEND: You shouldn't be concerned about the relations [between things] but about the things themselves, in isolation. Nothing more antipoetic than the logical relation between two objects of whatever type! One must break the bonds that relate things visibly and invisibly; one must permit objects and concepts to wander freely wherever they want to, and to fight and fly, so that the world can be more amusing and true poetry can exist. You poets have a horrible fear of losing your head, and an incomprehensible love for the logical quality of things. It is absurd for you to suppose that a shoe can only serve as a shoe and a spoon as a spoon. The shoe and the spoon are two forms of extreme beauty and have their

own life, as intense as yours. And above all they have a capacity for adventure that you can hardly imagine.

POET: Oh, I see, I can turn the shoe into a little boat or...

FRIEND: No! No! The shoe is nothing more than a shoe, without your inventing a new personality for it. A shoe that can fly away with an olive or a nose, into the Southern Sea, on the simple emotion of the breeze.

POET: I understand. It is one more poetic fact.

FRIEND: No, poetic, no, *real*, extremely real, and alive. Poetic of course, because everything is poetic, but alive, without fantasy, like an ant, like a spurt of water. Poetic facts are enclosed in books and never break out. What I'm talking about is what can be seen with the eyes. I have seen a donkey with the head of a nightingale and a huge wave like three water lions, pulling up in fear before a grain of salt. (*Poemas en prosa*, ed. Anderson, 91-92; Anderson 2004)

By fall 1928, when Lorca gave his lectures on "Imagination" and on the "New Painting" in Granada, both Dalí and Buñuel had criticized him harshly for his *Gypsy Ballads*—a book that, according to Dalí, contained disappointingly conventional notions of the object, was incapable of "moving us and satisfying our modern desires," fell "fully within the traditional," and was tied "hands and feet to the old poetry," i.e., to traditional metaphor and imagery of a sort readily accessible to logic. Clearly, Dalí had now moved far beyond the ideas which Lorca had expressed in the "Ode" and in "St. Lucy and St. Lazarus," painting canvases and writing prose poems ultimately inspired by the aesthetics of collage: the removal of objects from their usual contexts; the unsettling juxtaposition of strange, invented things like flying breasts, gadgets, severed limbs and torsos; and the creation of new objects combining parts of old ones—for example, the "donkey with the head of a nightingale." Stung by Dalí's rejection of the *Ballads* (whose popular success seemed to align Lorca with the *putrefactos*), the poet too had begun to move in a new direction, toward the *hecho poético* ("poetic fact" or "poetic event"), a term he seems to have borrowed from Dalí: the freestanding image *not* based on metaphor and occurring like a miracle, outside the normal—i.e., metaphorical—course of poetic events. Aware of the limitations of "traditional" verse (the eight-syllable ballad) and metaphor that could be solved like a riddle, and turning to "instinct, chance, pure inspiration, the fragrance of the direct," Lorca had written a series of prose poems influenced by Dalí's paintings of 1927-1928, as well as an unorthodox "Ode to the Most Holy Sacrament," which he had dedicated to one of his artistic mentors, the composer Manuel de Falla. The prose poems responded, he told his friend the critic Sebastià Gasch, to "my new *spiritualist* manner, pure, raw emotion, unleashed from the control of logic, but—careful! careful!—with a tremendous *poetic logic*. They are not surrealism, careful! The clearest *consciousness* illuminates them" (EC 588). To another friend he wrote that he was creating "a vein-opening poetry, a poetry which has *evaded* reality, with an emotion that reflects all my love of things and all my humor about things" (EC 587). In December, 1928, he remarked in a newspaper interview that he believed in a return to inspiration and to instinct: "I cannot bear logical poetry. The lesson of Góngora has already been learned" (OC 111:366). None of this would have mollified Buñuel, who had been criticizing Lorca—and his effect on Dalí—for the past year or so. For Buñuel, the *Gypsy Ballads* were only "approximately" modern. "There is dramatism, for those who enjoy this sort of flamenco dramatism. There is the soul of the classical ballad for those who like prolonging, one century after another, the classical ballad. There are even magnificent and extremely new images, but only rarely, and mixed with a plot or theme (*argumento*) that has filled with menstrual blood every bed in Spain" (letter of Sept. 14, 1928, in Sánchez Vidal, 180). To Buñuel, both the "Ode to the Most Holy Sacrament" and the prose poems were failures. "You understand the distance there is between you, Dalí, me, and all our friends who are poets," Buñuel wrote in February 1929 to Pepín Bello—a confidant of Lorca and Dalí from the Residencia days.

> They are two antagonistic worlds, the pole of the earth and the south of Mars, and every one of [those poets], without exception, inhabits the crater of the most stinking putrefaction. Federico wants to do Surrealist things, but they are false, made with the intelligence, which is INCAPABLE OF FINDING WHAT INSTINCT CAN FIND. As an example of his latest piece of bad work, see the fragment published in the *Gaceta*. It is as "artistic" as his "Ode to the Holy Sacrament," a foetid thing that will give an erection to the soft member of Falla and those of all other artists. Despite everything, within the hopelessly traditional, Federico is one of the best, perhaps the best, who exists. (Santos Torroella 1992, 223)

There is no record of Lorca's reaction to Buñuel's relentless hostility, but one can imagine the pain he must have felt—and probably tried to hide—upon receiving Dalí's letter. Days later, he wrote calmly to Gasch: "Yesterday Dalí sent me a long letter about my book [...] A sharp, arbitrary letter that poses an interesting poetic issue. I know that the *putrefied* have not understood my book, although they say they have" (*EC* 585).

*

Although Lorca would not have defined himself as an orthodox, practicing Catholic, and Dalí was to declare himself "anti-religious," at different moments in their lives both turned for aesthetic inspiration to the Catholic liturgy and to the lives of saints and martyrs, whose miracles bore a vague analogy to the *poetic facts* or *events* he and Dalí began to talk about in 1927 (*See* "Imagination, Inspiration, Evasion", p. 161). For Lorca, the Catholic Mass was a poetic manifestation of the deepest possible mystery: when he spoke, years later, of creating a stage version of a series of traditional ballads, he thought of the way the Mass gives enduring form to human sentiment, and what he wanted on stage, he said, was a "distant evocation," the "plastic algebra of a drama of passion and pain," as in the Mass (*CP* xl). Some of his works—for example, parts of the *Lament for Ignacio Sánchez Mejías*—draw their rhythm and tone from the liturgy, whose parallelistic structure, also found in the traditional lyric, was deeply embedded in his own poetry. Dalí would have understood the aesthetic resonance of hagiography and liturgy, but would remain a religious skeptic. "You are a Christian whirlwind," he once wrote Lorca, "and you need my paganism." The friendship with Lorca, he once wrote, was based on "the violent antagonism of [Lorca's] eminently religious (erotic) spirit and my own anti-religiosity" (Gibson, 1999, 100). The art critic Sebastià Gasch has told of sitting one night with Dalí and Lorca at a café table in Barcelona. Suddenly, Lorca "told his friends he had to go home early so that he could attend Mass the next morning at the cathedral.

> Smiling softly, [Lorca] rolled his dark eyes skyward and murmured something about the "aroma of ancient pomp" he always experienced inside the huge Gothic church. Dalí pointed toward the table where they sat and said, "I'm more interested in this olive." (Stainton, 150)

Of all Catholic martyrs, it was probably Saint Sebastian whom Lorca and Dalí invoked most frequently—in letters and conversation, poems and drawings—as mediator of the debate between modernity and tradition, pathos and "asepsia." Sebastian's iconography would have been familiar to any Spaniard—a robust youth with a beatific expression, tied to a tree or column and transfixed by arrows. His story had been told in *The Golden Legend* by Jacobus de Voragine, whom Lorca is known to have perused. Born in third-century Gaul (Milan, according to some accounts), Sebastian entered the Roman army and was promoted by the emperor Diocletian—who did not, at first, realize he was Christian—to captain of the guards. When Sebastian revealed his Christianity, angering his master, Diocletian ordered his soldiers to fire arrows at him until he was dead. But Sebastian survived their attack, was nursed back to life by St. Irene (as in the famous series of paintings by La Tour) and was finally beaten to death in the Hippodrome.

Because part of their correspondence has been lost, it is impossible to know whether it was Dalí or Lorca who first broached the subject of the third-century saint, whose meaning they would discuss for several years. Lorca mentions him for the first time in April 1926, after seeing a small polychrome wood sculpture by Alonso Berruguete (ca.1488-1561) of a young Sebastian, tied to the trunk of a tree, in the National Museum of Sculpture in Valladolid, where Lorca had been invited by his friend Jorge Guillén to give a poetry reading. Within months, he had turned Sebastian into a symbol of poetry, and had decided to give a series of three lectures (never written) on "The Myth of Saint Sebastian," with slides of Berruguete's saint "and other famous ones": those of Guido Reni? El Greco? Ribera? Mantegna? "I like your poems very, very much," he writes to Guillén, after asking him to send a reproduction of the carving by Berruguete.

> They are chaste and profound. They are an invitation to astronomy. The reduced sea and jelly sailors of much of recent poetry, drown in this monotonous, pure, "hard green water" which runs like a marble frieze to the eternal, lovable place of true poetry, which is love, effort and renunciation. (Saint Sebastian) (*EC* 170)

The phrase, "an invitation to astronomy," would have come from Dalí, who meant it as the antidote of all that is hackneyed, vulgar, rotten ("astronomy" was the opposite of "putrefaction"). As for "love" and "effort," they are easily associated with Lorca's vision of poetry: "Poetry doesn't need skilled practitioners," he remarked in a 1928 lecture. "She needs lovers, and she lays down brambles and shards of glass for the hands that search for her with love" (162). What he meant, in 1926, by "renunciation" is a little harder to specify. The renunciation of facility like that shown by Rafael Alberti, to whose "jelly sailors" he alludes in the letter to Guillén? In his lecture "Play and Theory of the *Duende*," given years later, he was to insist that the artist must renounce skill and security in order to battle hand-to-hand with the demon of inspiration (*SD* 53). Or perhaps by "renunciation" he means abstention from all that would distract him from poetry? When Lorca began to write, he embraced Romantic notions of poetry and music as spiritual callings akin to religion. "The World" was the poet's enemy; to write, one had to renounce it. Why St. Sebastian should be an emblem of poetry is another problem. As a symbol of passion? Of receptivity to the "arrows" of the poetic imagination? John Ruskin had spoken of the "imagination penetrative," the "penetrating possession-taking faculty Imagination," which works "not by algebra, nor by integral calculus; it is a piercing pholas-like" (Kaye 1999, 282). But in 1926, Lorca was not thinking in terms of Ruskin's piercing mollusk: in his lecture on the Baroque poet Luis de Góngora (1926), or in the "Ode to Salvador Dalí," it is the *creator*, the *poet* who fires the arrows, not the imagination; "[I] sing the firm direction of your arrows," Lorca writes of his friend. On Góngora's nocturnal "hunting trips"—on his search for the image in the dark forest of the imagination—he "fires his arrows only at the best images," ignoring the inferior ones (*DS* 72-73). To the Lorca of 1926, the best artist—Góngora, Guillén, Dalí—is also the best bowman or marksman. What he is emphasizing is the active element—not the passive—in the process of artistic creation. It was not until later that Lorca would equate the state of poetic receptivity with a sort of vulnerability: the "poet is a man who is always—because of everything!—on the point of tears" (*DS* 3). No one who does not make himself vulnerable—to human suffering, to death, to irrational impulses—will ever write a single line of true poetry. Sebastian also came to represent the poet's vulnerability vis-a-vis his audience. In 1932, reading *Poet in New York* in public, sharing the most difficult poems he had ever written with "the huge dragon" of the audience, Lorca paused to comment: "Let us agree that one of man's most beautiful postures is that of St. Sebastian" (*PNY* 230).

It was, specifically, the lyric poet whose vulnerability seemed best represented by Sebastian. "[Sebastian] poses," Lorca writes Dalí, "he uses his body to lend eternity to whatever is fleeting, giving visible form to an abstract aesthetic idea, just as the wheel gives us the consummate idea of perpetual motion. That is why I love him."

No doubt, as they traded letters, drawings, and allusions to Sebastian, Lorca and Dalí were keenly aware of the intensely erotic meaning of their saint, and of a "penetration" both figurative and physical. In the nineteenth century Sebastian had become a "gay icon," fostering "associations of feminized masculinity, homoerotic desire [...] and sado-masochism, all seemingly sanctioned by religious faith." So writes Richard A. Kaye, who has studied the saint's identity in Victorian times. As one example among many, Kaye points to Oscar Wilde: "Adopting the accoutrements of Roman martyrdom as a badge of honor, Wilde chose the name of Sebastian Melmouth as his *nom de voyage* on departing for Paris after his 1897 release from Reading Jail" (Kaye 1999, 269-70). According to Kaye, Wilde and his contemporaries were reacting to Renaissance visions of Sebastian as "a handsome youth pierced with arrows, in which the martyr is evidently at peace or even deliriously content with his punctured state. [...] Sebastian probably held homoerotic significance throughout the fifteenth, sixteenth, and seventeenth centuries, where his close relation to the Emperor Diocletian probably contributed to his reputation as a homosexual saint" (273). Like a gay male concealing his sexual identity, Sebastian had kept his Christianity hidden. His "coming out" had led to death.

"In my 'Saint Sebastian' I remember you," Dalí writes to Lorca in 1927, alluding to an essay on aesthetics he had just written (141-150), "...and sometimes I think he *is* you... Let's see whether Saint Sebastian turns out to be you." Lorca does, in fact, pose as St. Sebastian in more than one drawing and photo he sent to the painter. But the role of Sebastian passed back and forth between them. Decades later, in his *Secret Life*, Dalí remembered an early unconsummated heterosexual encounter which had placed him "under the sign of St. Sebastian": love, he discovered, was *receiving* the arrow and not firing it, and he experienced in his own flesh a "Saint Sebastian" from which he would never free himself (Gaillemin 60). Telling an interviewer about his relationship with Lorca, Dalí remarked, hoping, as always, to provoke his listener: "He [Lorca] was a pederast [sic], as everyone knows, and was crazily in love with me. He tried twice to [...] me. This was greatly embarrassing since I wasn't a pederast, and I could not yield. Besides, it hurt. And thus the thing never took place. But I felt extremely flattered from the point of view of prestige" (Bosquet, 69; omitted word in the original). Lorca was no "pederast"—what Dalí is claiming is that Lorca had attempted to sodomize him. If this is true—and until Dalí's death he insisted it was—the painter would have thought of himself as Lorca's "St. Sebastian." "Turns out that Sebastian is the patron saint of Cadaqués," Dalí writes Lorca in 1926, and adds that he had heard a story about Saint Sebastian "which proves how tied he was to the column and how solid his back was. // Didn't you ever think how strange it is that his ass doesn't have a single wound?" Ian Gibson believes the final line was meant as a taunt: Lorca had never been able to "possess" his unwilling friend. If this is true, Sebastian would symbolize, as he did in the late nineteenth century, a figure who inspires passion without returning it, the object of love who receives the gaze of male—and female—admirers while staring blissfully or ecstatically *elsewhere*. As Kaye (1999, 291) puts it, the Sebastian that had taken hold at the *fin de siècle* represented "not so much homoerotic affection as the ability to induce, without submission, erotic affection in others."

"Oh Desolate heart, / Cupid's Saint Sebastian!" Lorca once wrote (CP 247). But no doubt, for poet and painter, the saint's symbolism went beyond poetry and Eros. Sebastian has long been regarded as a protector against disease. His occasional role, today, as an advocate against the ravages of AIDS, reminds us that, from the Middle Ages into the

Renaissance (when St. Roque, St. Anthony and others took his place in Spain), the protection of St. Sebastian had often been invoked against the plague, and his penetrating arrows had been associated not only with the darts of love, but with those of infection (in earlier times, love itself was regarded as a *mal*, a disease, spread by the rays of vision), so that it is not surprising to hear Dalí allude to the saint as protection against the "germs" of emotional "putrefaction," and as a symbol of artistic "asespsia," of irony (solvent of emotion), and objectivity (*See* "St. Sebastian"). Renaissance painters had often rendered him, in the midst of his suffering, with an impassive or beatific face, and that, too, must have attracted Dalí, in his flight from emotion. Sebastian seemed a spiritual "straight man," as unaffected by pathos—physical or emotional—as Langdon, Keaton or Menjou. Lorca's take on that impassiveness was somewhat different: he admired Sebastian's "serenity in the midst of misfortune," specifically, as a symbol of the artist—perhaps of any man—criticized by society because of his sexual orientation. "All of us are a little like St. Sebastian when they criticize and gossip about us. He sinned against his epoch," and, in that sense, his death was logical. He is a "fresh-water myth," Lorca adds:

> Isn't it true that St. Sebastian is far, far from the sea? Isn't it true that neither waves nor mountains can hope to understand him? St. Sebastian is a fresh-water myth in a glass of pure crystal. It was indoors that he became a martyr, not lashed to a gnarled tree trunk the way the Romantic Renaissance portrayed him. He was tied to a column of jasper as yellow and translucent as his flesh.

The figure of Sebastian tied to his jasper column (as in versions by Mantegna and "Il Perugino"), "far, far from the sea," will remind readers of the *Gypsy Ballads* of St. Michael, patron saint of Granada, whom Lorca depicts as an "ephebe," an effeminate archangel closeted in "the alcove of his tower," dressed in spangles and lace. A somewhat similar contrast—between fresh water and the ocean—occurs in Lorca's "Ode to Salvador Dalí," written in 1926. Alluding to the seascape of Cadaqués, Lorca writes: "The sirens convince, but do not compel, / and they come out if we offer them a glass of water." In Dalí's poetics, during the years he was closest to Lorca, the ocean symbolized an infinite Nature—associated perhaps with Romantic, heterosexual love—which he hoped to bring under the dominion of art. Alluding to that struggle, Dalí reports to Lorca, one afternoon, that he is painting waves:

> All afternoon I have been painting—seven hard cold waves like the ones in the sea. Tomorrow I'll paint seven more. I feel calm because I have painted them well and every day the sea looks more like the one I am painting.

There is an echo of the letter—or of the idea behind it—in Lorca's "Ode":

> Hygienic soul, you live on new marbles, / fleeing the dark thicket of incredible forms. / Your fantasy reaches as far as your hands / *and you enjoy the sonnet of the sea in your window.* (italics ed.)

No doubt, Lorca associated these very phenomena—the retreat from the elements; the conversion of a boundless natural world into the most controlled of artistic forms—both with Dalí and with his native

Granada, a timid city where, he said, man has always fled from nature—wind, driving rain, ocean, stars—a city whose love of small, intimate things has found refuge from the elements in the interior courtyard, the convent or monastery, the salon, the tiny chamber, or the walled house and garden (*SG*). The man from Granada —like the Dalí of the "Ode" or the narrator of "St. Lucy"—would ask not for a starry sky but for a single star framed in the window. In Dalí's world in the "Ode", "a desire for forms and limits overtakes us," one similar to the desire felt in Granada:

> ...to limit, enclose, bring indoors, and place in our hands objects and ideas which seem too large: time and space, the sea, the moon, distances, and even action. // We don't want the world to be so big, the sea so deep. We need to limit and domesticate anything huge. (*SG* 63)

Granada was the antithesis of Seville, city of love and adventure, of Don Juan (*SG* 67). There, too, lay a sort of renunciation. The "jasper column"—supremacy of art—rather than the gnarled tree trunk (work of wind or wave). One of Lorca's letters to Anna María Dalí in 1927, reminds us that, although the renunciation of nature was a source of spiritual strength—it produced an admirable contemplative tradition—it could also lead to a certain sexual emptiness. "The señoritas of Granada have no love of the sea," Lorca wrote ironically to Dalí's sister. "They have great mother-of-pearl shells with painted seascapes, and that is the way they see it. They have huge conch shells in their drawing rooms, and that is the way they hear it."

That sexual emptiness—desire that burns to sterile ash—was a theme Lorca was to explore in *Doña Rosita the Spinster*, staged in Barcelona in fall 1935, an occasion which brought the playwright back into contact with Dalí for the first time in years. Ian Gibson, who has written biographies of both the painter and the poet, describes that meeting.

> On the night of 28 September [Lorca] was to have participated in a poetry and musical recital given in his honour. The hall was full, the orchestra ready, the choir lined up; expectation was mounting ... but Lorca's admirers waited in vain. The charismatic poet had gone down the coast to Tarragona with Dalí, with no explanations given. (*Shameful Life*, 406-07)

The two of them spent happy hours together and, later, with Gala, Dalí's companion and muse; and Lorca told a journalist that he and the painter were planning new projects together: "We are twin spirits. And here's the proof: seven years without seeing each other and yet we agree on everything as if we'd never stopped talking since then. Salvador Dalí is a genius, a genius" (Gibson, *Shameful Life*, 407). Less than a year later, in the opening days of the Civil War, Lorca was brutally murdered in Granada. Dalí remembered feeling a certain exhilaration. "Olé!" he exclaimed, "using the term in its bullfighting sense of admiration for a brilliantly executed pass: Lorca, obsessed by death, had fulfilled his destiny to perfection" (*Shameful Life*, 418). The memory of Lorca would haunt him for the rest of his life, and one can imagine him re-reading, or merely remembering, the letters, drawings and poems Lorca had sent him in his youth. Many of those letters—it is impossible to know how many—are now lost. The mementos which remain, and which are gathered here, bring back a time of love, friendship, and intellectual "fencing," when each artist made himself vulnerable to the other's desire. Arrows fixed forever, wounds which never healed.

Christopher Maurer
Boston University, 2004

Salvador Dalí

The personality of Federico García Lorca produced an immense impression on me. The poetic phenomenon in its entirety and "in the raw" presented itself before me suddenly in flesh and bone, confused, blood-red, viscous and sublime, quivering with a thousand fires of darkness and of subterranean biology, like all matter endowed with the originality of its own form. I reacted, and immediately I adopted a rigorous attitude *against* the "poetic cosmos." I would say nothing that was indefinable, nothing of which a "contour" or a "law" could not be established, nothing that one could not "eat" (this was even then my favorite expression). And when I felt the incendiary and communicative fire of the poetry of the great Federico rise in wild, disheveled flames, I tried to beat them down with the olive branch of my premature anti-Faustian old age, while already preparing the grill of my transcendental prosaism on which, when the day came, when only glowing embers remained of Lorca's initial fire, I would come and fry the mushrooms, the chops and the sardines of my thought...

The Secret Life of SalvadorDalí

Federico García Lorca

Dalí, who is imponderably marvelous, has sent me some charming poetical pieces. Every day I feel his talent more strongly. To me he seems unique. He possesses a serenity and a clarity of judgment and thought that are truly moving. He makes a mistake and doesn't even care. He is alive. His keen intelligence comes together with a disconcerting childishness in a mixture so unusual it is absolutely original and captivating. What moves me most about him just now is his delirium for construction, that is, for creation. He tries to create from nothing and makes such an effort, setting off with bursts of confidence and with an intensity that seems incredible. Nothing could be more dramatic than this objectivity, this search of joy for its own sake. Remember that this has always been the Mediterranean canon. "I believe in the resurrection of the flesh," says Rome.

Dalí is the man who fights off phantasms with a hatchet of gold. "Don't tell me about the supernatural. How odious St. Catherine is!" says Falla.

> Oh pure lance without a knight!
> How my light dreams
> Of your twisting path!

That's what *I* say. But Dalí refuses to be guided. He has to do the steering himself, confiding in his own astral geometry.

He moves me. Dalí fills me with the same pure emotion (and may the Lord forgive me!) as does the Christ child, abandoned in the manger at Bethlehem with the germ of the crucifixion pulsing under the hay of his cradle.

Letter to Sebastià Gasch, January 1928

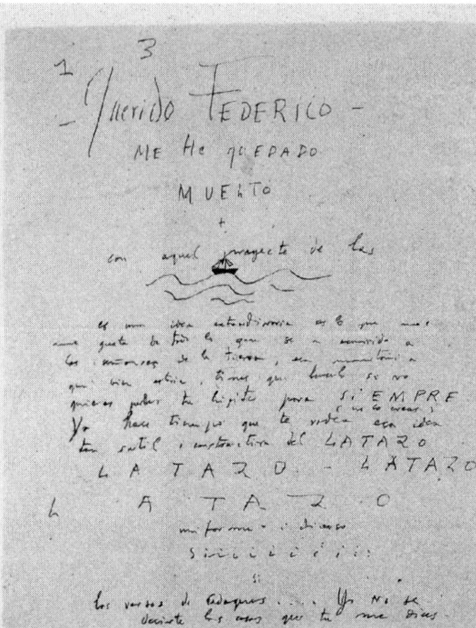

VIII,1

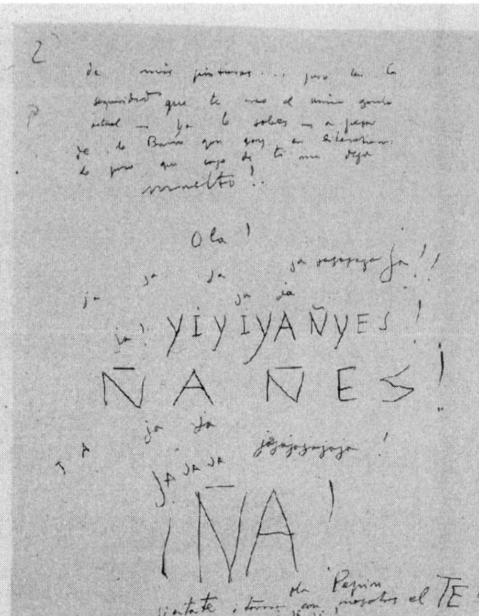

VIII.2

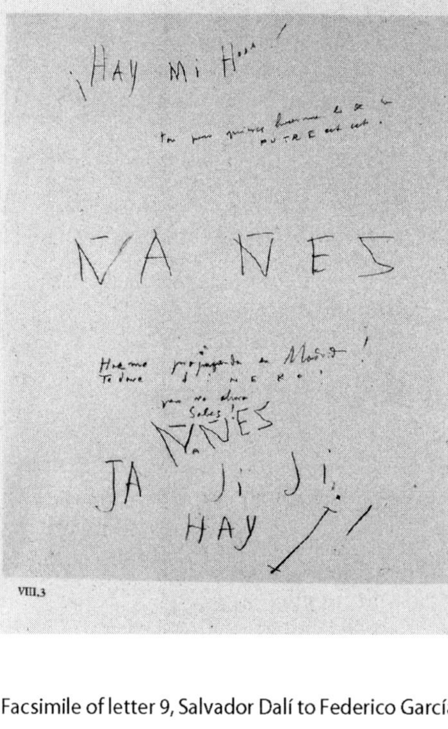

VIII,3

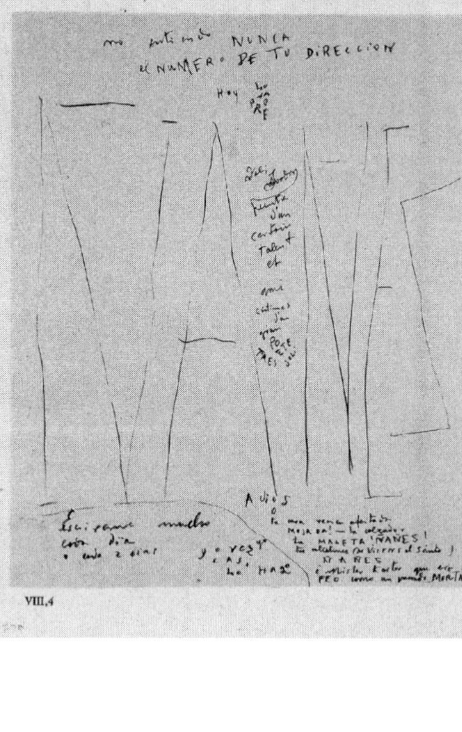

VIII,4

Facsimile of letter 9, Salvador Dalí to Federico García Lorca

Letters

1. FGL to Anna María Dalí

[Madrid, May? 1925]

Dear friend,

I don't know how I have the nerve to write you these lines. Ah, the shame of it! The shame, the Shame, the *Shame*, the SHAME! My shame will rise like that until it bursts into light beside the luminous Citroën of the Eiffel Tower. But I know you will forgive me. Every day I've thought of writing you. So why didn't I? I don't know, I guess I remembered you *more* that way, though you probably think I've forgotten about you completely. By the seaside, under the olive trees, on the avenue of Figueras, and in the dining room of your house under the Divine Shepherdess, I have an unforgettable portfolio of memories of you and your smiles. Besides, I never forget. Sometimes I write to no one, but my intensity never varies... (here a fly has dotted the 'i'—let us respect his opinions and help).

How is your Auntie? No matter how often I ask your brother this, he never answers. And your father?

I think of Cadaqués. The landscape is present and eternal and perfect, and the horizon rises up constructed like a huge aqueduct. The silver fish come out to bathe in the moonlight and you are probably dipping your tresses in the water, as the gas-powered launches stutter to and fro. When you're all in the door of your house, the afternoon will come to light the coral that the Virgin holds in her hand. There is no one in the dining room. The maid has probably gone off to the dance. In the window and the door, the two black ballerinas of white and green glass are dancing the sacred dance that scares away the flies. And then my memory settles down into a chair and eats *crespell* and red wine. You are laughing and your brother is buzzing like a golden bumblebee. Under the white porches, an accordion is playing.

Teresa *la Bien Plantada* is knocking on Lidia's door, but no one answers. The two "brave fishermen of Culip" are crying, their voices on their knees. Lidia has died. Anna Maric, at that moment I would like to hear the noises from the chains of all the ships pulling up anchor on all the seas... but the noise of the mosquito catchers and of the sea keeps me from doing so. Upstairs, in your brother's room, a saint hangs on the wall. Puig Pujades with his globe on his belly makes his way down the stairs. I am too lonely in the dining room, but I can't get up. One of Salvador's drawings has entangled my feet. What time can it be? Just now I would like to eat a little piece of *mona*. How do you say *nublo? Nub...* Filing by the window, crying bitter tears, is a string of those dusty women in mourning who are on the way to the notary.

—

And so I find myself in your dining room, señorita Anna Maric. My memory grows intense. Do you remember how you laughed to see my torn gloves the day we were almost shipwrecked?

I hope you will be able to forgive me. Forget about revenge. My sisters keep on asking "what you're like."

Remember me to your father and Auntie.

For you, my fondest memories.

FEDERICO

Will you answer me?

2. SD to FGL

[second half of June, 1925]

My distinguished friend:

The drawing of the white mantilla is without a doubt the most accomplished thing of yours I have ever seen. Your letter delighted me with its infinite photographs and infinite *states* and made me remember the good times we've had.

My sister, too, is delighted with your letter and will answer you soon.

Here I have a formidable gramophone and a huge stock of UNDREAMT OF blues. But I'll stop because this sort of literature makes me nervous and [illegible.]

SALVADOR DALÍ

3. SD to FGL

[Cadaqués, mid-July 1925]

Dear friend,

For many weeks I've been in Cadaqués. It's very calm here and I'm working hard. It has done me much good to get back to my olive groves. It was, after all, a return to nature.

I'm devoting much thought, just now, to the construction and architecture of the landscape. I think painting still has much to learn from Cézanne's grand ambition—"faire du Poussin d'après nature."

*

Our house has held on to a little of your precious friendship. This year the Divine Shepherdess of Cadaqués has blossomed once again on the white wall. Every morning this Andalusian "Rousseau" cheers me up and reminds me of our rooms and our poplars at the Residencia de Estudiantes.

*

I would like to have the addresses of Guillermo de Torre and of Halffter.

Your friend,

SALVADOR DALÍ

My address: C. Llané, no. 1, Cadaqués

4. SD to FGL

[Cadaqués, summer 1925]

Dear Federico:

I'm painting in Cadaqués. And I'm *still* enjoying the "Divine Shepherdess."

Did you do the poem about her you promised?

Remember me to your brother and sisters. For you a big hug.

DALÍ

5. SD to FGL

[Cadaqués, end of July/beginning of August 1925]

Dear friend,

Your letter brought me happiness and joy.

"The Iron Butterfly" seems to me to synthesize marvelously all thought about modern painting, where everything should have the same consistency and eternity (though not the same quality).

After *fauvisme*, figures that stand. And there's nothing as marvelous as feet pressed to the earth under the "weight" of the body. In Egypt, better than in Poussin, we find both feet on the ground. Xenius understood this, but on the way from Egypt to the Mediterranean, Polyclete added the "grace" of the free leg. That's why, when she is at rest, La Bien Plantada puts her weight on just one foot.

*

When I paint, I paint without shoes because I like to feel the earth very close to my feet.

I'm trying out some things with the goal of constructing the atmosphere, or rather constructing the void. I'm taking a great deal of interest in the plasticity of hollows, though it has never interested anyone; this plasticity almost always comes from solids.

I'll keep you informed as to the results of my experiments.

I'm awaiting your poems, for which I'm very grateful.

Remember me to your brother.

For you a hug.

SALVADOR

6. SD to FGL

[Cadaqués, summer 1925]

Dear Federico:

I can't come, can't abandon the paintings I've begun. *You come here!*

Tell me when you get here.

We'll publish your books in Barcelona.

*

Grosz (German) and Pascin (French) have already tried to sketch putrefaction. But they've painted—for example—the Stupid Gent with hatred, with rage, with malice, in a *social* sense. And so they've merely scratched the surface, barely capturing his most superficial elements. They've barely managed to distinguish The Stupid Gent from one less stupid. You and I are different—we've raised the Stupid Gentleman—and idiocy itself—to a lyrical category. We have reached a lyric of human stupidity, but with an affection and a tenderness toward that stupidity that is almost Franciscan.

The difference

The Stupid Gentleman of Grosz repels us, we hate him.

As for ours, we *adore* him, he brings tears to our eyes, we could kiss him. He's not our obsession but our joy.

In short, once again, our Mediterranean Sea.

Say hello to your family, and for you a big hug from your

DALÍ

¡Hasta pronto!

When do I get to read the entire "Ode"? You shouldn't be doling it out one drop at a time.

7. SD to FGL

[Barcelona, end of November 1925]

Dear Federico,

The exhibition has been a total success, both in reviews and in sales. They gave me a banquet, etc. etc.

The *harshest* criticism is the one I'm enclosing. The others are devoid of interest, they're unconditionally enthusiastic.

*

What are you up to? What are you working on? Please don't stop writing. You're the only interesting man I've ever met.

I suppose you received a letter by way of Barradas. You have no idea how intense life was during the exhibition.

Remember me to yours, and for you a big hug from your

DALÍ

[dedication on drawing:]

For García Lorca with all the tenderness of his little child DALÍ 1925

8. FGL to Anna María Dalí

[Granada, beginning of September? 1925]

Dear friend Anna Maric:

In Granada I've just received your delightful letter. I haven't forgotten you, ever, and if I haven't written until now it wasn't my fault... it was because of the crazy days I spent in Madrid. Now, in Andalusia, I'm another person, the same one I was in Cadaqués. How often I've remembered that near shipwreck we had on Cap de Creus! And how delicious, that rabbit we ate with salt and *sand* at the foot of the orange-colored eagle. That sea is my sea, Anna María.

How lovely what you tell me about my poor gloves (which someone loaned me so that I could look more presentable in your house). Truly lovely.

Hats and gloves seem to soak up the whole personality of the person who has worn them. Give me someone's glove and I'll tell you his character. In the attic at Casa Pichot there are probably gloves from the entire family—black, calfskin, little white gloves from First Communion, knit gloves... it's probably incredible to see them in a wicker basket... above all, mothers' gloves, and the sound of the sea! I don't even want to think about this theme from Ibsen. Let's remember Niní, who, dressed like Orpheus, comes along singing like a drunken sailor on a tin shell.

You say that you have spent a delightful summer and that makes me happy. A summer of motorboats and classical gestures. As for me, I've had a rather bad one. I have worked hard, but I yearned to be by the sea. And then I was, and cured myself completely. I can say that Málaga restored me to life. And thus I was able to finish my *Iphigenia* (I'll send you a fragment).

The business about Lidia is charming. I have her portrait on my piano. Xenius (Count of...what was it?) says she has the madness of Don Quixote... and here we must roll our eyes and clench our teeth: he's wrong! The madness of Don Quixote is a dry, visionary madness of the high plain, an abstract madness *without images*. The madness of Lidia is *plastic*. Don Quixote rides through the air, and Lidia roams the shores of the Mediterranean. There's the difference. And I want to put this into circulation so that Xenius's slip doesn't get established. How admirable Cadaqués is! And how amusing to compare Lidia and the last knight errant! Will you forgive me for this little comparison between one temperament and another? I think so, for we have often talked about these things. And above all we have been able to save our rrrare folks, our rrocks and rrooks and the rrrich.

You had never met [Ernesto] Halffter? Isn't he an interesting fool? He is enough of a *fool* to become a great artist. Why don't you and your brother come to Granada? My sisters will write inviting you. Say hello to your Auntie and your father. I have so many things to thank them for. Remember me to Salvador, and know that I will not forget you.

FEDERICO

And a friend of eternal Cataluña, always!

Visca!

Anna Maric, what do you think of the portrait of your brother? Write and tell me. Don't forget this poor shipwrecked Andalusian sailor!

9. SD to FGL

[Figueras, end of February/beginning of March 1926]

Dear Federico:

Your project of the [drawing of boat and waves] really kills me.

It's an extraordinary idea, the best that ever occurred to any earthly mortal.

It would be wonderful, that monotony, you've got to do it, unless of course you want to lose your little son FOREVER (don't believe me). For a while now you've been interested in that subtle, instructive idea of doing something that's a HUGE BORE.

A BORE A BORE A BORE

Uniform and diverse.

Yesssssssssss!

Yes.

Ah, those lines about Cadaqués! As for what you say about my painting, I don't know how to respond, but believe me, I consider you the only true genius in the world. You already know that.

Despite the fact that I'm a donkey, a donkey in literature, the little bit of you I *do* manage to understand just kills me.

Hello! Ha ha ha ha hahahaha Ha ha ha! BOO-BOOBY! BOOBY! Ha ha ha aha.

Hi, Pepín, take a seat and have some TEA with us!

Hee hee.

AY, my "Ode"!

And you're not even doing the PUTREs for me?

BOOBY

Promote me in Madrid!

I'll give you *money*, but not now. You know? BOOBY Hah! Hee hee! Ay!

I NEVER understand the number in your address.

Today I'll try it out.

BOOBY

DALI SALVADOR *peintre d'un certain talent et ami (intime) d'un grand POÈTE TRES JOLI.*

Goodbye.

Ay, your newly-shaved face when it's still WET. Your shoehorn and your SUITCASE

BOOBY

And your socks (of St. Vicens)

BOOBY and Mister Carter, uglier than mortal sin.

Write me every day, or every two days.

That's what I do, almost.

The marriage of BUSTER KEATON

in New York [Collage: *See,* Color Gallery]

Goodbye, Federico, write a long long letter to your DALÍ SALVADOR

And time went by...

AND BUSTER AND NATALIE RECEIVED THE NUPTIAL BLESSING

Sainte Vierge Marie

Reigne du ciel

priez pour nous!

10. SD to FGL

[beginning of 1926]

LYON. OUR LADY JOAN OF ARC HAS BEEN PROCLAIMED PATRON SAINT OF WIRELESS TELEGRAPHY

(From the newspapers.)

Dear Federico,

I am getting postcards from Paris from Vicens, Buñuel, Moreno Villa, Hinojosa. Instead of Miares, *Select American Bar,* Montparnasse.

It seems that Buster Keaton has made a movie at the bottom of the ocean with his little straw hat on top of his diving bell.

Long live the rose on its bush!

Soon I'll send you the drawings you asked me for, together with a bookplate for you and a wonderful cover for your book *Songs*.

A huge hug

SALVADOR DALÍ

11. SD to FGL

[Barcelona, beginning of March 1926]

Greetings, dear sir!

I've spent the entire Sunday afternoon rereading all of your letters. My dear, they are extraordinary! Every line suggests numerous books, plays, paintings, etc. etc. etc.

My God, what a fat, cute little Japanese you are!

If I've understood anything in poetry, it's this:

> A *harsh* crown of white brigantines
> binds bitter brows and *hair of sand.*
> *The sirens convince but do not suggest,*
> *and they come out when offered a glass of fresh water.*

This is fantastic. It is almost ARITHMETIC.

Before, I used to like things with sharp contrasts, distant relations, strongly realistic, like these lines of Cocteau speaking of life in the trenches:

> Car ici le silence est fait
> avec tout: de la glaise, du plâtre,
> du ciment, des branchages secs, de â tôle
> des planches, du sable, de l'osier.
> *Du tabac, de l'ennui*
> *des jeux de cartes.*
> Silence de stéréoscope,
> de musée Grévin (1), de boule

en verre il neige, de chloroforme,
d'aérostat.

Marvelous, right? But you rise above that in ordinary conversation.

*

...Noël me donne le vertige,
m'angoisse l'âme avec douceur,
comme descendre en ascenseur.

Isn't that purely impressionistic when we compare it to your things? In poetry I think no one has known how to get beyond mere *sensation*. And they throw in a bit of humorism so as not to seem so Romantic. By contrast, in these verses of yours, the only things in play are concepts.

That sense of

Saturday, garden gate... etc. etc.

but in [the lines] *a hard crown of wh...*, etc., there is no sensation of anything, just comprehension, abstraction, anti-putrefaction.

Am I getting it?

*

I'm waiting for your suggestions about putrefaction so we can bring out our little book right away. *It would be great if you could come immediately!* What would you say to including "Buster Keaton's Stroll"?

I can promise you the edition will be immaculate.

I know you're working on it. I know I'll receive it tomorrow, day after tomorrow at the latest, or *are you no longer moved by my little putrefied people?* Remember your room at the Residencia, remember PEPÍN!

NCAAÑRETSER

JAFISS

It's not fair I can't see my "Ode"!!!

I'm not *that* much of a donkey, I'll understand *some* of it.

OK, goodbye goodbye goodbye goodbye

How nice Lidia's letter is when she says, commenting on the *photograph,* that I was standing between culture—that is, philosophy on the right and woman on the left.

What a wonderful definition of culture!

Goodbye.

DALÍ

The photos of the painting are bad, very bad, you have no idea *how much better the painting is in person,* but no matter how little you imagine, this will give you an idea. Look at the geometrical *foundation,* the *composition,* which is the basic thing about the painting. It is constructed with *diagonals.* Order above everything.

CLARITY!

(1) Wax museum

12. SD to FGL

[Figueras, mid-March 1926]

Dear Federico,

I'll draw all of the covers you want for any magazine you tell me to, but you have to be more specific and give me the facts:

size

black and white or color, etc.

degree of putrefaction of the magazine.

*

I see, sadly, that the photo and the prologue still haven't gotten here. You're capable of not doing it! What a pretty, spoiled little gentleman you are!

My gentlemen no longer move you. But just think it would be an exquisite edition, printed on Japanese paper.

Ay!

You don't even have to mention my drawings, just give an idea what putrefaction is. Five pages, for God's sake, for the Mother of God do it, don't write me again without sending it, I can't *believe* you don't want to sit down and write about this, for me!

*

Everything you tell me seems extraordinary—the train without wheels and the exacerbated sensibility of Braque—seems certain and incontestable (cannot be contested).

Ay!

Who else tells me the things you do? NO ONE!

Believe me, sir, the greatest painter that ever was is Vermeer of Delft. I may have mentioned that in another letter.

I am painting a "Girl in Figueras." For the past five days I've painted devotedly, patiently, the back of her newly shaved neck, and it's coming out very well, *so well* that it almost doesn't *look* (though it is) modern (or old.)

You remember my Swami? He's dead.

I'm sleepy.

Your thing about the *lady* seems too cerebral.

My Swami and Pepín.

Adolphe Menjou is a great film actor, the one psychologically closest to Pepín. He played the saxophone while his wife was in a rage. Remember?

I don't have *attacks* of anything.

Send me the prologue and your photo so I can paste it up behind me in the aeroplane.

I'm more your little son than ever.

You are a strange, religious spirit. You're strange. I can't relate you to anything of known proportions. Ri ri ri ri ri ri ri ri cccc.

And I don't like the insect books of Fabre.

Creecrreeee

Rac rac rac RAC CAR

Yes sir!

No sir!

Nor do I understand Margarita [Manso] at all. Was she stupid? Crazy?

I'm reading *Le bal du Compte d'Orgel* of Radiguet. Child child child my my my, how good it is!

Daddy, daddy, daddy Lebonard. How far we can go, eh?

Fween fween fween yyyy

This could go on forever, couldn't it?

Look, an I with lots of dots on it

i.........

And another, with even more dots.

i.............

What's his name? Antonio Moreno.

"Antonio Moreno," remarked Moreno Villa, biting his mustache.

Think of *that*! What things!

Look, now I'll draw you an O

O

An O

Think of *that*.

Dear Federico, I can't write any more because I HAVE NO PEN. Look how affectionately I'm going to write your name. I'll do the whole thing in one breath.

Federico Garcia Lorca

and now I sign

SALVADOR DALÍ

Do you love me?

Note. *Send me the prologue,* or *else*… me me me mic mic mic

Another i with lots of dots on it, and dots of lots, so you'll be happy. I'll draw it up here, but down here there wouldn't be room for so many dots. Look, here it is. I.......... So many dots, right?

Come to Figueras, *tout de suite.*

Think of this. If Fortuny were alive today and were to open a drawing and painting school, every avant-garde painter would attend. At least I would.

13. SD to FGL

[Cadaqués, beginning of summer 1926]

[...] Some other time I'll tell you about St. Objectivity, who now goes by the name of St. Sebastian.

Cadaqués is a "sufficient fact," and to go beyond that is excess, a venial sin. Excessive profundity could be worse, could be ecstasy. I don't like liking anything extraordinarily, I flee from things that can send me into ecstasy, like automobiles. Ecstasy is a danger to the intelligence.

At seven when I begin to paint is when the sky does its extraordinary, dangerous things, and instead of contemplating the almost always unbearable spectacle of nature, I take my Charleston lessons at the home of the Salisacs. That dance is perfect, since it perfectly impoverishes the spirit.

How good I feel! I am in full Resurrection, it's like Easter! That business of not feeling the anguish of giving oneself to everything, that nightmare of being submerged in *nature*, that is, in mystery, in what is confusing and inapprehensible—settled down finally, limited to a few truths and clearly ordered preferences which satisfy my spiritual sensuality.

Mr. Professor tells me: but nature too has its order, its laws, its *superior* measures.

"Superior," dangerous word! It means superior to us, an order incomprehensible to us, mysterious laws and measures, and from there we get to religion and principles of faith and occultism and Papini with his fast, wanting to write an encyclopedia.

But thank God, it is perfectly clear today where art begins and where naturism.

Goethe, such a good thinker, used to say that nature and art are two different things. Le Corbusier knows about that, and about love [...]

14. FGL to Anna María Dalí

[Lanjarón, August 1926?]

[...] The Mediterranean is one and indivisible. I'll tell you a story about the aesthetics of Lanjarón. A boy was being beaten by his parents. And they took away the grapes he was eating. And they ripped his clothes to shreds. The boy ran out of the house crying and ran into another child. The second one asked him, "Why are you crying like that." The tearful boy answered, "Come to the top of the hill and I'll tell you." And they went walking off to the hill, and when they reached the top the boy who wasn't crying said, "Ok, now tell me what happened," and the other boy started out, sobbing: "Well, my parents beat me, etc. etc. etc." When he had finished telling about his pain, the other boy stared at him and said with annoyance: "Is that all?"

The Mediterranean is one and indivisible.

My mother is much better. I'm dying to go to Cadaqués. But I don't know whether my family will let me. I don't know. I would like to escape. [...]

15. FGL to Anna María Dalí

[Granada, August 1926?]

Dear friend Anna Maric,

I've taken a while to answer you because for several days I've been staging a magnificent *attack* of fever and I've had to give it all the attention it deserved.

It began with the most delicate sort of trembling, like a *tempo rubato* from Chopin, and this I turned into a serious, marked rhythm with the object of scaring my family and making them rush up and down the stairs in great excitement. It turned out very well.

Truth is, I was sorry it wasn't caused by cavities, for these are the most sumptuous, the best organized, the most alarming episodes, and they have no complications. This one has been intense, and has left me yellow, with my ears like paper. It's over now.

*

Since the weather has been good, the young ladies of Granada go up to the whitewashed miradors to see the mountains and *not* look at the sea. The blonde ones are in the sunlight and the dark-haired ones in the shade. Those with chestnut-colored hair are on the first floor looking at themselves in the mirror and putting on celluloid combs.

In the evening they dress in gauzes and vaporous silky things and they go to the promenade where they can listen to diamond fountains and ancient torments of roses and melancholies of love. Later they stuff themselves on pastries and bonbons from a store which ought to be known as "Paris, France" but is really called "The Bird Cage." The social life of Granada is prodigious with poetry and lyrical putrefaction. The flora of the Mediterranean blossoms here with all of the delicacy of its marvelous greys. Cactuses and olive trees. But the señoritas of Granada have no love of the sea. They have great mother-of-pearl shells with painted seascapes, and that is the way they see it. They have huge conch shells in their drawing rooms, and that is the way they hear it.

Blessed are you, Anna Maric, both siren and shepherdess, dusky with olives and white from the cold foam. Daughter of the olive groves, cousin to the sea!

*

I'm a little annoyed with Granada. I want to leave this place. Sometime, perhaps soon, I'll have the pleasure of seeing you.

Until then, the best friendship of

FEDERICO

The beasts are coming!

Did you see how many beasts went to the homage for Rusiñol?

YES.

16. SD to FGL

[September 1926]

Dear Federico,

I'm writing you with great calm and serenity. Let me explain. We've already had some bad weather in this blessed September, it's raining, it's windy, a boat is anchored in the harbor, and all this makes one more aware of being inside, with the rustle of gentle, quiet labor... My sister is sewing bed sheets or tablecloths at the window by my side and in the kitchen they're making buns and talking about putting out grapes to dry. All afternoon I have been painting—seven hard cold waves like the ones in the sea. Tomorrow I'll paint seven more. I feel calm because I have painted them *well* and every day the sea looks more like the one I am painting.

Turns out that Sebastian is the patron saint of Cadaqués. You remember the hermitage of Saint Sebastian on the hill at Pani?

Well, Lidia told me a story of Saint Sebastian which proves how tied he was to the column and how solid his back was.

Didn't you ever think how strange it is that his ass doesn't have a single wound?

But let me leave all this and answer your letter about situations, for the two of us are already old friends.

You're not going to take qualifying exams for anything. Persuade your father to let you live in peace without all that stuff about *assuring your future*, working, *making a personal effort*, etc. Publish your books, they can give you *fame*, America, etc., with a *real* name and not the *legendary one you have now*; anyone but an ass would put on any play you write, etc. etc.

I dream of going to Brussels to *copy* the Dutch painters in the museum there. My father likes the idea. Visit you in Granada? I won't kid you, I can't. Sometime around Christmas I have to put on my exhibition in Barcelona, which is going to be really special. Child, I have to work hard between now and then, just as I am now, the whole day without thinking of anything else. You can't imagine how I've given myself to my paintings, with what affection I paint my windows open to the sea with rocks, my breadbaskets, my girls sewing, my fish, my skies like sculptures.

Goodbye, I love you very much, someday we'll see each other again, and what a time we will have!

Write me! Goodbye, goodbye. Off to my dear paintings.

SALVADOR DALÍ

17. FGL to Anna María Dalí

[Granada, November 1926?]

Dear Anna María:

I've been hearing rumors that your brother has gone off to France, and other such bits of news which, naturally, I don't believe. Since he had agreed to send me some drawings for my books and never did, perhaps he *has* made a little excursion to our neighbor to the north. Tell me the truth about all this, and dispel those rumors.

At home we've been greatly annoyed because we haven't heard in over two months from my brother, who is in Paris. I'm working hard. In my first book I dedicate one of the songs to you. I don't know if you'll like it, but I've made sure it's one of the prettiest. Answer, and if your brother is there tell him not to be so lazy, for I need his drawings.

Remember me to your parents and friends. Goodbye, Anna Maric. Friendship and affection from your friend and Little Fool

FEDERICO

Acera del Casino, 31, Granada

18. SD to FGL

[Figueras, 18-20 January 1927]

Dear Federico,

I've spent almost a month in Barcelona because of my exhibition, and I'm glad now to be back in Figueras, with a new stock of phonograph records and infinite old and new things to read.

And with many paintings at my *fingertips*, and *not* in my head.

As you can see, I'm writing to invite you to my new type of Saint Sebastian, where the arrow is transmuted into a flounder [138]. The principle of elegance is what made Saint Sebastian suffer and die so deliciously well. It was anti-elegance that led him, like a coward, to convalesce. But it had to be that way. For now, I want you just to accept this. Perhaps in this new change we will once again find the true temperature of the arrows of the old Saint Sebastian.

Blessed Rigol has told me about you and much else. I hope you really *are* about to publish your extraordinary books.

*

Did you get a *Gaseta de les Arts* with reproductions?

*

Goodbye. Remember me to the *select* folk at *Litoral.*

When can I find out about you? Why don't you write me a little?

The other day in Hospitalet, Barradas showed me a "clown-ist" portrait of you and Maroto. I almost cried. What a stupendous Suchard chocolate little Japanese you are!

SALVADOR DALÍ, 1926

19. SD to FGL

[Figueras, early March 1927]

Dearest friend,

At last I've found some truly good writing paper, and I'll be able to write you more comfortably and at greater length.

What you're asking me for is crazy. What a stupid title, *El Gallo del Defensor*. I pick up my pen and send you the rooster and everything else you wanted. But I'm sure that everything I'm sending will be useless, because once it reaches your hands it will begin to get lost and diluted in the pores of your marvelous dissociation. Ah!

You won't believe this, but for the past month I've been a soldier. I haven't mentioned it until now because it's a very long story, but anyway I love it, it's so strange. I can't even *think* about traveling for now. But this summer we'll have to spend three months together in Cadaqués. It's fate. No, not fate, but it *is* a sure thing.

Tell me what you think of my literature. I just say whatever occurs to me, the product of my physics and metaphysics.

Goodbye.

DALÍ

How could you ever think I *don't really like the Dutch painters?* When you see what I'm doing now, you'll realize you're wrong… but

*

Back to the first letter.

I can't send you the article yet because I'm taking out one part and adding other things. Clearly my true vocation is painting, but anyway I think I'm saying things.

I'm longing, mon cheri, for a very long letter from you. In my "Saint Sebastian" I remember you and sometimes I think he *is* you... Let's see whether Saint Sebastian turns out to be you. But for now let me sign in his name.

A great hug from your

SAINT SEBASTIAN

Mantegna.... irony!???

I'm sending you dumb little things for *gallo*. I don't believe in "adorning" anything, and neither do you, but these are inventions more than "adornments."

Why don't you want to have anything to do with irony? In my article I speak precisely about that and defend it. Irony—nakedness—seeing clearly, limpidly, discovering the nakedness of nature that, according to Heraclites, *likes to conceal herself*. That's irony. Paint all the waves in the ocean. Irony!

20. SD to FGL

[Figueras, early April 1927]

Dear Federico,

I see that your *Marianita Pineda* is going to become a reality at last. My father is delighted. The whole family will go to the premiere. My father also tells me that if within two months you still haven't published anything, he is going to write you a terrible letter.

I'm very sorry to be tied up in the army. If the premiere were to be very soon it would be materially impossible for me to do the stage settings. If I were to take responsibility for them it would be to do the best I know how, and naturally, with enough time, even though I have a perfect idea of their plastic realization.

It goes without saying that something as pure as your *Mariana Pineda* shouldn't be done with a stupid stage setting. Of all the people we know, only Manuel Ángeles Ortiz or I could do it for you.

General indications for the settings of Mariana Pineda:

Every scene, framed in the white frame of the lithograph you were planning. With that white frame, in addition to the title, there could be a verse, which would change with each act.

The curtains could be mere backdrops for the figures, with filigreed plastic indications of the stage. The color must be in the costumes of the characters. So that the characters can achieve maximum visibility, the decoration will be almost monochromatic. The very slight changes in tone must be like fading. All the furniture, cornucopias, consoles, etc., sketched very simply in the setting. The clavichord, cut from cardboard and painted the same as the other furniture. But all the glass must be real (don't you think?)

The whole setting will have such simplicity that it won't upset even the swine, because the impression it will make when the curtain goes up and before the play begins will be one of absolute calm and *naturalness*.

Besides, unfortunately, there are already too many people who tolerate those things. Here every Tom, Dick and Harry is afraid of looking stupid and everyone says they want people to think them intelligent.

Note for the setting of *Mariana Pineda*:

To take maximum emotional advantage of the very slight chromatic changes in the setting.

21. SD to FGL

[Figueras, early May 1927]

Sir!

I have your letter and telegram. I'm going to Barcelona on the 19th or the 12th, I'm not sure yet, and I don't know if I'll have any money. At the moment I have 600 pesetas (a little painting, that little marine life that you liked, sold to a widow who has a house in Naples), and this is what I have to go to Barcelona to spend, for I need a couple of barroom days before I begin the summer. But you know that I spend that much in a single night. I don't even have enough to dip my peseta notes in whiskey. If you have money you could come to Barcelona to get me. By plane it would be a matter of hours. If I manage to sell some things I have in Dalmau that seem eminently saleable, I'll take the plane myself, but if not, I don't even have enough for Miss Pierrette (no, no, no drama, not yet!) I bought that sweater that I was pining for in El Siglo, remember?

Hello, why are you still in Madrid, you happy little rooster?

We need our acts of madness, our foot traffic, our weeping, our laughter, our hunger!

There are street fairs here where they take faded photos of the faces of beasts. And what about my poem? What scorn you show for it. It was fantastic.

Remember me to Margarita [Manso?], she's probably a big girl by now.

*

I'm growing strong from boxing and am very tan. Yesterday I was in Cadaqués with all its putrefied beasts weighing on my heart, and its fine sand, of which there is very little. Ah, but you'll get frightened of the plane and won't come.

Goodbye. What the hell are you doing in Madrid? Are you thinking of going on with the Xirgus?

If only we had 3,000 pesetas we could spend a marvelous week!

22. SD to FGL

[Figueras, beginning of June 1927]

Dear Federico,

In about four days I'll get three months of leave and we can be together without any rush or bother.

Ah, foolish little child, why was I dumb enough to hide my *true enthusiasm* for your delightful *Songs*? It's just that a number of things occurred to me—things that seemed "inadequate" (as you say), things seen from a superficial but pure modernity (but merely a plastic modernity).

Any song of yours (all this is mere impression on my part) appeals to me more than the purest line of poetry in the *Thousand and One Nights* and more than any popular song, but it appeals to me *in the same way*.

The poetry in the title of any Charleston from America (for example, "Let's Have Another Piece of Pie") or the new poetic unity caused by objects invented totally anew, top to bottom, just a couple of weeks ago, appeal to me *in a totally different way*.

I think no epoch has ever known the perfection of ours. Until machines were invented, there had never been anything perfect, and man had never seen anything as beautiful or poetic as a nickel-plated engine. The machine has changed *everything*. Our age is as different from others as the Greece of the Parthenon is from the Gothic. One has only to think of the badly made, ugly objects that existed before technology. We are surrounded by perfect, novel beauty, which brings about new states of poetry.

We read Petrarch and see him as a consequence of his age: the mandolin, the tree full of birds, the old tapestry. He uses materials from his own age. I read [your] "Orange and lemon" and I get no feeling for the painted mouths of manikins. I read Petrarch and I *do* sense his ample bosoms decked with lace.

I look at Fernand Léger, Picasso, Miró, etc., and know that machines exist and new discoveries in the natural sciences.

Your songs are of a Granada with no trolleys and still without airplanes. They are an old Granada with natural elements, far removed from today, purely popular and constant. "Constant," you will tell me, but that "constant eternal" element you all talk about takes on a different flavor in each age. Some of us live in new ways from the same "constant" elements, and that is the taste we prefer. (But you will do *whatever you want to*, that goes without saying).

All this is my own taste, and probably it isn't perfect. I am superficial, and the outside of things is what delights me, for in the last analysis the outside of things is the objective. Today objectivity is what I like most in poetry, and only in the objective do I see the trembling of the ethereal.

Yessir, I know, I'm just babbling, writing you without any control whatsoever, and I need to set this down more meticulously and calmly. When we talk, something always gets cleared up. But at any rate you will catch my intention, for you are capable of seizing my ideas, even the dumbest, most confusing ones I have.

Lots of love. Hasta pronto.

DALÍ

23. FGL to SD

[Barcelona, late July 1927]

My dear Salvador,

When the car pulled away, the goose began to cackle and tell me about the Duomo of Milan. I wanted to throw myself from the car so that I could stay with you in Cadaqués, but was stopped by Pepe's expressive wristwatch and nose—the nose he used to cook every morning in a Parisian double boiler, with a hard little coral of blood on his pitiable face [?] As I lost sight of the Qucurucuchs and we turned onto the highway you looked very small, gobbling up a little red oily hand using a tiny plaster fork that you were removing from your eyes. All of this with the tenderness of a newly hatched chicken [...]

Now I am sweating and [...] unbearable heat. Cadaqués has the joy and neutral permanence of the place where Venus was born but *where no one even remembers.*

It approaches pure beauty. The vineyards have disappeared and each day there is more wave-like wheat and wheat-like waves. One day the moon will dip itself in those waves, supple as a fish, and the church tower will rock back and forth over the hard *pitiable* houses: houses of quicklime or chewed bread. It's exciting to think of you discovering Cadaqués and I remember Salvador Dalí the neophyte licking the shell of the sunset without waiting to go inside: pale, rosy shell of a crab on its back. But now you're inside. What anguish, my child! Even here I can hear the gentle whoosh of blood from the bleeding Beauty in the Forest of Apparatuses, and I hear the crackling of two little beastlings, like the sound made by peanuts when you crush them in your hand. The woman cut to pieces is the loveliest possible poem about blood. There is more blood there than was spilt in the Great War, for that was *warm* blood, and its only use was to *water* the earth and quench a symbolic thirst, all eroticism and faith. Your painterly blood and the whole plastic conception of your physiological aesthetics has such a tangible, well-proportioned, logical air, and such true, pure poetry, that it reaches the category of *what we cannot live without.*

One can say, "I was feeling tired and I sat down in the cool shadow of that blood," or "I went down the mountain and ran the whole length of the beach before I found that melancholy head, the locus of all the delicious crackling beastlings that help us digest our food."

I realize now what I've lost by our separation. Barcelona gives me the impression that everyone is playing and sweating and intent on *forgetting.* All is confused and bold, like the aesthetic of the flame, and everything is indecisive and unhinged. But in Cadaqués people stand firmly on the ground, aware of all the sinuosity, aware of every pore in the soles of their feet. Here in Barcelona I understand why, in Cadaqués, I used to be able to feel my shoulders. I love to remember the slippery curves of my shoulders and how, for the first time, I felt the blood coursing through them, in four sponge-like tubes that trembled like a wounded swimmer.

I would like to cry, but with the unselfconscious tears of Lluis Salleras or the stupendous singsong of your father humming the sardana

Quina llagrima.

I have treated you like an indecent mule—you, the dearest thing that I have. I see this more clearly by the minute and feel truly repentant, but that only increases my affection for you and my loyalty to your thought and your humanity.

Tonight I will eat with all our friends in Barcelona and toast to you and to my stay in Cadaqués (the express was sold out).

Give my best to your father, to your sister Anna María, whom I dearly love, and to Raimunda.

Remember me when you are at the beach and above all when you paint crackling things and my little cinders. Oh my little cinders! Paint my name into the picture so that my name will mean something in the world, and give me a hug, for I badly need it. Your

FEDERICO

It's very hot!

Poor little fellow!

Don't forget the article about my exhibition, and write me, my child!

24. FGL to SD

[Barcelona, Madrid or Granada, August 2-11? 1927]

[...] drunk. I never saw anyone crazier. He said, "Dalí ought to do an exposition with a prologue by you."

[Josep] Dalmau said of you, "He is superior to Picasso in imagination," and [José María de] Sucre answered through his rotten teeth, "Picasso and everyone else." Dalmau begged me to leave my pictures in the gallery until Picabia got there, he wanted him to see them. Antonieta says he showed them every day. I gave Dalmau the "Water Drop," and he gave me a complete set of brushes and oils, which he'll send to me when he sends the pictures.

I think of you and your little house. And I have never thought more intensely than now. It's really the limit. I hope you'll write me. I'll answer telling you things about the *Forest* and all the rest. And you'll tell me whether you are a little resentful and whether you've erased me from your friendship.

Tell your sister nice little things, and for you a big hug from your

FEDERICO

Write me!

I'm sending you these drawings, which aren't good, but which will help me do others that I want to do.

25. FGL to SD

[August 1927]

My dear,

It had never occurred to me that Saint Sebastian's arrows could have colored feathers. His arrows are made of steel and the difference between you and me is that you see them fastened in him—fixed, stout, short arrows *which never grow rusty*—and I see them as *long* ones, at the very *moment* they have wounded him.

Your St. Sebastian is made of marble, the opposite of mine, who is continually dying, and that is the way it has to be. If my St. Sebastian were too *plastic,* I wouldn't be a lyric poet but a *sculptor* (not a painter). I needn't explain to you why I wouldn't be a painter. The distinction is a subtle one. What moves me about St. Sebastian is his *serenity* in the midst of his misfortunes. Misfortune has always been Baroque. I am moved by his *grace* under torture and by the absolute lack of *recognition* he shows in his Hellenic face. He is not *resigned* but *triumphant,* someone who has triumphed, filled with elegance and different shades of gray, like a steady, faithful oarsman oblivious to the avenues of the city. This is why St. Sebastian is the loveliest figure in all of art, *the art seen with the eyes.*

Isn't it true that St. Sebastian is far, far from the sea? Isn't it true that neither waves nor mountains can hope to understand him? St. Sebastian is a fresh-water myth in a glass of pure crystal. It was *indoors* that he became a martyr, not lashed to a gnarled tree trunk the way the *Romantic* Renaissance portrayed him. He was tied to a column of jasper as yellow and translucent as his flesh. The tree had been invented in the Middle Ages.

All of us are a little like St. Sebastian when they criticize and gossip about us. They were truly right to put St. Sebastian to death: his martyrdom was truly right and just, at least in those days. He sinned against his epoch... without even realizing it (the aesthetic of the scale). No martyr ever *did* realize it. And all of them were martyred for political reasons. They didn't die for having adored their own god, but for not having respected everyone else's god. They were outlaws and they were wrong. In a pinch, perhaps Socrates would have chosen to respect the laws of the Republic. What a dramatic conflict! St. Sebastian attained salvation because of his beauty and all the others because of their love. All of them made their martyrdom into a prayer, but St. Sebastian was different. He poses, he uses his body to lend eternity to whatever is fleeting, giving visible form to an abstract aesthetic idea, just as the wheel gives us the consummate idea of perpetual motion. That is why I love him.

The breeze that reaches us from the sea is thin and delicate. Birds can fly in it without carrying a set of *spare wings* as they do in the Pyrenees or in the Caucasus. Here at the hotel there is not a single shapely calf. The girls who come up from the waves simply *look* and those who come down from the mountains *desire*. I feel isolated and don't want to speak to anyone except the waiters (who are very handsome), for I already know what they're going to say. I remember you always—too often. It is as if I had a gold coin in my hand and didn't know how to let it go. Not that I *want* to let it go, dear child. To love you more I imagine that you are very ugly. [...]

26. SD to FGL

[Figueras, end of September or beginning of October 1927]

My dear,

You drank yourself sick? I'm living a life of the utmost virtue—I don't drink at all—*absolute* chastity. Vice is totally *artistic*. Every morning I spar with the soldiers and we build stamina with long runs. When night comes, and it's time for bed, it's delightful to feel that tiredness, which is different for the small-minded and miserable.

Write me, I have no idea what you're up to. What are you doing about the magazine?

My dear little pictures, pure, newly born, are to be exhibited for the PUTREFIED of Barcelona.

Goodbye, write me, if you ever remember. You know I'm at your service.

DALÍ

I'm writing in a lot of different places, and soon I'm going to begin to write a DAILY article.

Goodbye. I like that.

As always, I'm happy.

27. SD to FGL

[Fall, 1927]

Dear child,

Overjoyed to hear you're impressed by Miró. Miró has said something new, after Picasso. I don't know if I told you, I'm in contact with him, and that he came to Figueras and will soon return to Cadaqués to see my latest things. He has an enormous *purity* and a great *soul*. He thinks I'm much better than all the young people in Paris, and he writes saying that everything is marvelously ready for me to be a great success there. You realize *he* has been a huge success at selling his things.

Don't tell anyone, but I think I'm doing *really great things*. I paint with true fury. I work hard at a line or a dot, erase it, and remake it a thousand times. Evasion of the customary, of the anti-real, conventional reality to which the art of swine has accustomed us. I feel hatred for almost everything in the museums, and rage about all that I've painted before yesterday.

I have the *intuition* that someday I'm going to say unknown things. Ugly things? Beautiful? Hah hah hah hee tee tee hee with a little hair me me Me me MMMMMMMMe me!

OK, I love you, and I'm good-looking as hell.

Don't you think the only poets, the only ones who really make new poetry, are us painters? Yes!

Just the opposite of what the word poetry means to Juan Ramón, Benjamín Palencia and other great SWINE. Miró paints little chicks with hairs, sex organs, etc.

You have to become the first new poet. I don't think there *are* any. Breton is *very* intelligent, perhaps more intelligent every day, but he's no good at poetry... and the chimney goes on belching smoke, and those who insist on removing that figure who was placed on a sort of beach.

Yours,

DALÍ

"Poem of the Little Things"

There is a pretty little thing that smiles and looks at us.

I'm happy, I'm happy, I'm happy, I'm happy.

The sewing needles sink sweetly into the little, tender pieces of nickel.

My girlfriend has a hand of cork, full of thumbtacks (black thumbtacks).

My girlfriend has knees of smoke.

Sugar dissolves in water, dyes itself in blood, and *jumps like a flea*.

My girlfriend has a wristwatch of putty.**

The two breasts of my girlfriend: one is a swarming wasp's nest, and the other a calm garrot.

The little sea nettles, little sea nettles, little sea nettles, little sea nettles, little sea nettles, sting.

The eye of the partridge is red.

Little things, little things, little things, little things, little things

Little things, little things, little things, little things, little things
There are little things as still as a loaf of bread.
Salvador Dalí,
October 1927

**tachuelas negras*—I don't know if that's the way one says it in Spanish
**Mastic—the soft stuff that people put on their windowpanes.

Like it? Write me. What's the matter? Goodbye. Soon I'll send you some verses that are to be sung like a Charleston, to the accompaniment of banjo and bugle entitled "the sweet nape of my girlfriend's neck has just come from the barbershop."

28. SD to FGL

[October-November 1927]

Federico,

I've just received the two most recent issues of *Verso y Prosa*. It's disgusting, the marasmus of putrefaction they're in, that whole generation of Prados, Altolaguirres, etc. How disgustingly arbitrary it is, and what rotten sentimentality there is beneath their pseudo-intellectualism. It pains me to see your things, so unique and true, lost in all that rubbish.

Soon you'll receive almost a whole book of my *poems*. Poetically I am the anti-Juan Ramón, who seems to me the commander in chief of poetic putrefaction. His putrefaction is the worst of all, and by his side, thanks to his bad taste, even that great vulgar pig Rubén Darío takes on a certain South American charm comparable to the architecture of the Casa Colom in Cadaqués.

Until now the metaphor and the image have been anecdotal. So much so that even the purest, most uncontrollable of images can be explained like a riddle. Anyway, I'm going to write you a long essay about what I think about poetry.

A hug

DALÍ SALVADOR

Goodbye. What did you think of the "Poem of the Little Things" I sent you?

Juan Ramón has never seen anything, he only feels putrid emotions about things.

Hello to Xirgu, the Muñozes, the Porredones, etc.

Remember me to the rubber Calandres, the cafés and bistros.

I've reread *Platero and I,* which I remembered as good. It's *nauseating,* all that emotional ecstasy before things he doesn't see, that he simply *doesn't see.*

29. SD to FGL

[Figueras, November 1927]

Dear Federico,

Here is my "poem" with photographs for *gallo*. Please take good typographical care of it and follow my directions. The numbers show the place the photos should go and the titles are: I: Butterfly; II: Hen; III: Special Face.

If it's difficult to use the photos because they're pasted down, you'll have to make another photo from these photos. This is easy, but without them the poem loses a lot, since it's something very organic and homogeneous. I think I've managed to capture something of reality, at least a tiny bit, far from the conventionalism and stylization of common poetry. It's a poem I thought long and hard about, and did with a "double decimeter" (and surely it's greatly inspired). I want you to like it. We have to let go of the poetic rot that is historical, anti-real and decorative, the rot we've inherited, and try to get away from our invented coherence and do so with the greatest aplomb and levity. At last poetry seems possible!

A big hug. Tell me what you think of the poem.

DALÍ

Please don't publish anything of mine without telling me. I demand more of myself every day, and can't stand what I did the day before yesterday.

Say hello to your friends for me.

As you can see, there's really just one photograph, which is *situated* in different ways. I think that gives it great homogeneity

POEM

Hair under the arm, the lips and
edge of the nose.
Edge of the nose, rotten beast of the
moon
Lips, edge of the nose and beach
belly button and wrinkle

FISH PURSUED BY A GRAPE

Dedicated to a conversation of Federico with Lydia

That fish and that grape were nothing but small little things, but they were rounder than others and wherever they went, they were very still.

Some things are like a comet, and when you move them, they leave everything wet.

That little thing was a star with a tail, and it was lying still on the table.

There are flat little things.

And little things that stand on one leg.

Others are a hair, and others had been salt.

The fish in question had been a small grain of salt, this small grain of salt was very bright and it was brought to Europe in the curly fur of an Eskimo coat, all by itself in the poopdeck of that yacht with the name of an island.

Another small grain of salt was now a fish, thanks to a very special check.

*

On the beach were eight stones—one liver colored, six moss-covered, and a very smooth one—and there was a piece of cork drying in the sun, and a hole in the cork where feathers were nesting. Beside the cork there is a slender reed split through the belly and placed on the sand. All of this together forms nothing other than a rapid, speedy cluster of grapes, the stones are its sweetness, the liver-colored stone its poisoned sweetness, the moss-covered one the six latest phonograph records, the cork its skeleton, the feathers its grains, the slender reed split through the belly the souls, and the smoothest stone—do I have to tell you?—was the most wrenching blues sung the other day by my girlfriend looking cross eyed and wrinkling her little nose like a small animal.

*

It was precisely that cluster of grapes, sunk to the bottom of the Cape of Champagne, which had just reminded me of the light of the California vineyards. I was trying to make the little fish understand, by means of the slight trembling of my cards (without interrupting my poker game with Baroness X) how in California, in the last days of August, the vineyards rustle toward sweetness, with a noise similar to rain falling on baby partridges. At that very moment, and perhaps because of the excitement produced in the jewels of the aforementioned Baroness by the momentary memory of origin of the little grain of salt of the fish, that the grape leapt up excitedly and began pursuing the grape, this thanks to a skillful transformation of the diamond in my fiancé's ring, which was running away, without being noticed, carried vertiginously in the automobile that I myself was driving.

Then the little grape decided to try out a different form of speed, which it had seen peach stones use during the long periods they have to spend enclosed in empty places, so that the grape began to shrink until it was a very, very tiny grape and soon there was only distilled grape residue, flying like a madwoman through the air, and a small constellation of buckshot.

*

There were more and more cars full of bandits pursuing us and firing at us, and the bandits were wearing small woolen caps and some of them, goggles for the wind.

The road was a flute with holes and in each opening there was a small rotting donkey.

*

We hear their engines nearby. We toss away the bottle of whiskey and the earth bristles with razor blades.

Eyes become grape pits. We hear the black gallop of their horses.

Two grape pits are a little grain of salt.

We toss away the tube of carmine-snow. We hear their sleds

skidding.

At last you have shed your dancer's suit, spangled with silver, and a wide sea with moonlight keeps us far from our enemies.

The little grain of salt wanted to be mistaken inside a windowpane.

Now, if you wanted to, we could resume the kiss interrupted in the dance hall, and make it last. But isn't it afternoon yet? Isn't the sun high in the sky?

Every blade of grass, even the slenderest ones has a side that is lit up, and another in shadow like the planets.

I know the exact place behind the house where there is a little dried-up beetle.

On a stone an olive is sitting still.

Don't you see? I am not crying, and yet, if I press on your fingers I'll crush the grape pits of my lunch and if I want to remember your legs I can't, unless I can take another look at that disturbing rotting donkey with the head of a nightingale.

The still olive is wearing little skirt.

For you I have a nice photo of New York.

SALVADOR DALÍ

30. SD to FGL

[Early December, 1927]

Federico,

I'm working on paintings that make me die for joy, I'm creating in a purely natural way, without the slightest artistic worry, and finding things that move me deeply, and trying to paint honestly, that is, *exactly*. In that sense I'm beginning to completely understand the senses. Sometimes I think I've recovered—with unsuspected intensity—the "illusions" and joys of my childhood. I feel a great love for grass, thorns in the palm of the hand, ears red against the sun, and the little feathers of bottles. Not only does all this delight me, but also the grapevines and the donkeys that crowd the sky.

Just now I'm painting a very beautiful smiling woman, *bristling* with *feathers of every color,* held up by a small marble dice that is *on fire*. The marble dice is supported, in turn, on a quiet, humble little plume of smoke. In the sky are donkeys with parrot heads, grass and sand from the beach, all about to explode, all clean, incredibly objective, and the scene is awash in an indescribable blue, the green, red and yellow of a parrot, an edible white, the metallic white of a stray breast (you know that there are also "stray breasts," just the opposite of the flying breast, for the stray one is at peace without knowing what to do and is so defenseless it moves me).

Stray breasts (how beautiful!)

After this, I'm thinking of painting a nightingale. It will be titled

NIGHTINGALE and it will be a feathered vegetal donkey in the woodsy canopy of a sky bristling with nettles, etc. etc.

Hello, dear sir! Yessirree, you must be rich. If I were with you I would be your whore to cajole you and steal peseta notes to dip in donkey piss...

*

I'm tempted to send you a piece of my lobster-colored pajamas, or better yet, "lobster-dream-colored" pajamas, to see if you are moved, in your opulence, to send me money. Don't you think it strange, dear child, that it hasn't even occurred to Xirgu to pay me even a little for my stage settings which after all, were a success among the putrified and—in Madrid at least—made the work much more avant-garde than it would have been if done by Fontanals or Alarma? Anyway, just think, with a little money, with 500 pesetas, we could bring out an issue of the ANTI-ARTISTIC magazine and *shit* on everyone and everything from the Orfeo Catalán to Juan Ramón.

(Give Margarita a kiss on the tip of her nose, the whole thing is like a nest of anaesthetized wasps.)

Farewell, Sir, a kiss on the palmtree from your

ROTTING DONKEY

Death to Juan Ramón's donkey (*Platero*), decorative stylized donkey, one of those anti-realistic donkeys which (as you know) are made from ant-covered cork, the same as glass.

31. FGL to SD

[Madrid, November or beginning of December 1927]

[...] Your latest things have the charm of a [illegible] *spinning face up. Wheels without a track* full of reality and good faith which carry out their mission revolving around a fixed point.

I can't understand why I need to look again and again at my fingernails while I read your poems. They make me feel as though a cat's hair had gotten into my blood, and I bring together indescribable things in the most amazingly natural way. The olive in a short little skirt is so joyous, so [...]

32. SD to FGL

[ca. January 15, 1928]

Federico,

I'm writing you in bed, where I'm recovering from two days of fever. I'm very bald and terribly good looking. When I get out of bed I will take care of the things you asked me for.

Soon I'll be out of the army and will begin to paint things to exhibit in Paris. I'm now firmly installed in a considerable *technique* that has allowed me to find *things* that are undoubtedly joyous and poetical.

A few days ago I went to Cadaqués to eat a great fish head with hot sauce and oil. Cadaqués was more *mineral* than ever, the olive trees rising directly from the smooth shale, like apparatuses, objectivity clenched its teeth and on the table top *a* smoke stood straight and peaceful as a bottlecap. The fish head had all the anatomy and patience of Mantegna, and all of the most golden olive oil of the best Tintoretto, and in the winter sun the breadcrumbs were at rest also, and some of them were sporting a little minute hand. The fabric of the towels (tablecloths) was magnified by the lens of the winter air of Cadaqués. As for Enriquet, whenever he spoke it was to say definitive things, and his big toe was cold as a glass of water. A slender eyelash is very beautiful too, and I was happy there were also little wrinkled things. The women who went to gather kindling all had their noses, a silhouette cast a little shadow on my hand, and a little button dangled by a thread from my sweater.

My father is going to do some remodeling and soon this house will be happier and more logical, without the dark corridor and there will be huge windows. You know there's no place I'd rather live.

PHOTOGRAPHY

I say to poets: I love bouquets of flowers because there is nothing closer to rotting donkeys. The bouquets of flowers painted by the watercolorists don't look like bouquets because they don't look at all like rotting donkeys.

No animal capable of greater *cruelty* and odiousness than the little dove.

No animal, on the other hand, more capable of tenderness than the hippopotamus.

*

I've just read the poems of Paul Valéry and the book that Paul Souday wrote about that swine.

Paul Valéry has all the signs of the worst sort of putrefaction. His intellectualism is the most boring imaginable. We must do without that *scum*. A Gide, above all *Si le grain ne meurt,* can have the intensity of an absurd personal case (mere biography) but he is incapable of interesting us. Gide is just another gigantic bore. We don't care a shit about his life, and at bottom he's the same as any vulgar songwriter and is incapable of moving us in a healthy way. In short: *Merde*!

Much affection

DALÍ

Gómez de la Serna is what the language of the people must become before very long. He is *witty, funny*.

It's just as much a miracle for an olive to be *at rest* as it would be for it to hop about.

Act of faith: Lorca, first true poet of the future when he purifies himself completely and becomes like a calm, beautiful little olive oil.

Cocteau? Unbearable. He just says pretty things.

Radiguet, better than Proust but useless.

PICASSO.

Photography, FILM = birth of poetry = the key!

First Poet of All: PICASSO

There are no poets who *write*.

The best of them *paint* or make *film*. *Buster. Harry Langdon.*

DALÍ

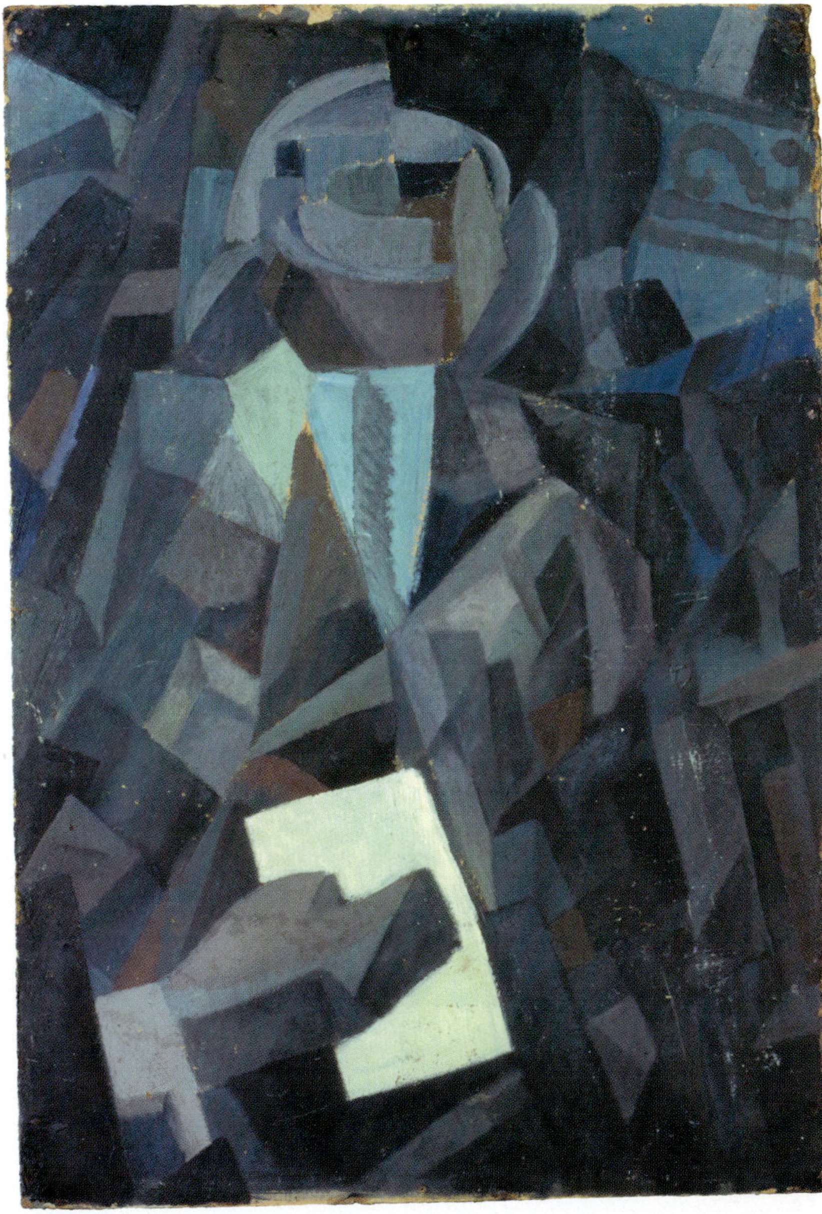

Salvador Dalí, *Cubist Composition. Still Life of a Person Holding a Letter*, c. 1923. Oil on cardboard, 74.6 x 52.1 cm. Gala-Salvador Dalí Foundation. The critic R. Santos Torroella (SD: *The Early Years*, 86) identifies the subject with García Lorca, a theory given credence by the study for this painting, where the manuscript in the figure's hand is entitled SUITE (perhaps alluding to *Suites*, a book of poems on which Lorca was working from 1921 to 1923).

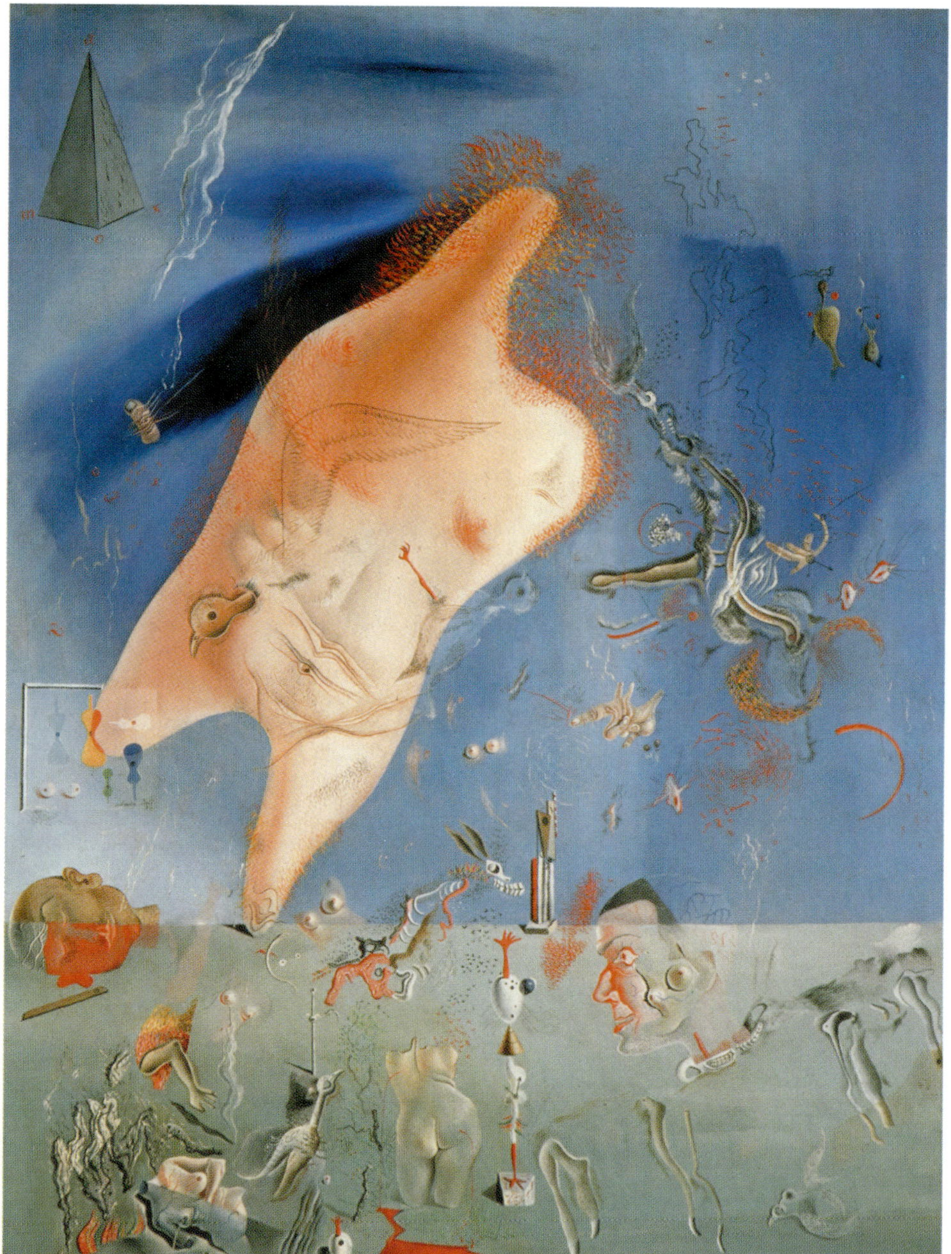

Salvador Dalí, *Little Ashes* (*Cenicitas*), 1928. Oil on panel, 64 x 48. Museo Nacional Centro de Arte Reina Sofía, Madrid.

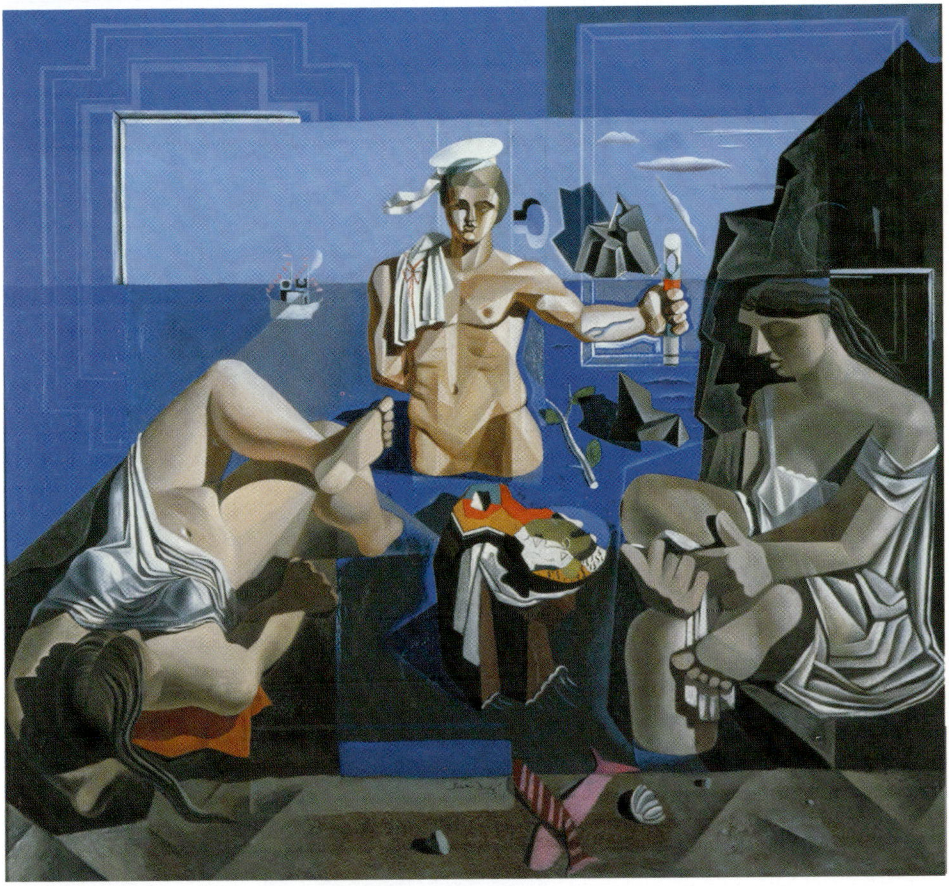

Salvador Dalí, *Academia neo-cubista* (*Neo-Cubist Academy*), also known as *Composición con tres figuras* (*Composition with Three Figures*), 1926. Dimensions and location unknown. Santos Torroella has noticed that the sailor in the center of the canvas bears a certain resemblance to St. Sebastian.

Alonso Berruguete (ca.1488-1561), *St. Sebastian*. Polychrome wood sculpture. National Museum of Religious Carving, Valladolid. The figure once formed part of the altarpiece in the convent church of San Benito el Real, Valladolid.

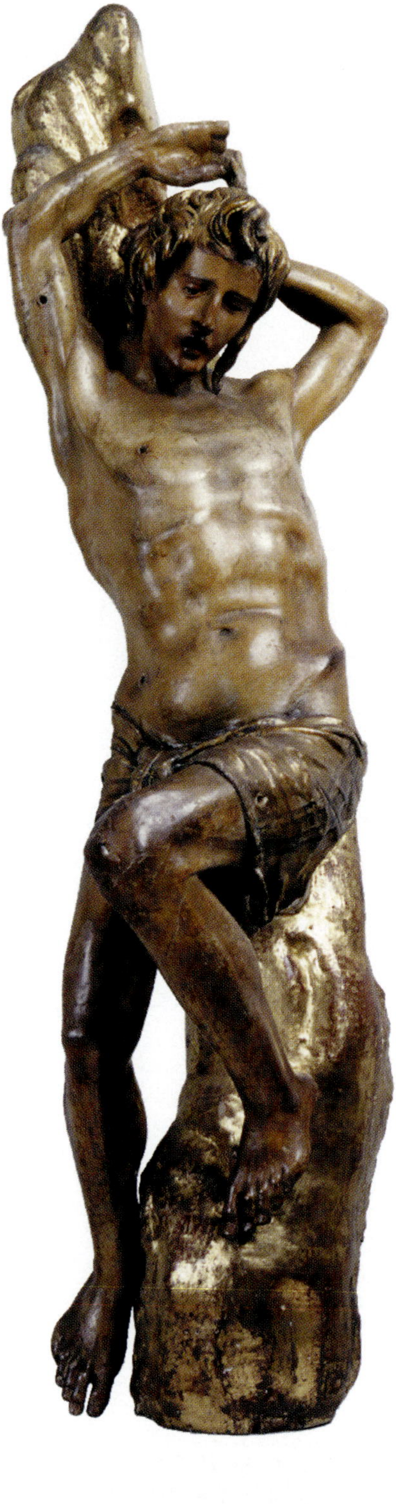

San Sebastián, Alonso Berruguete

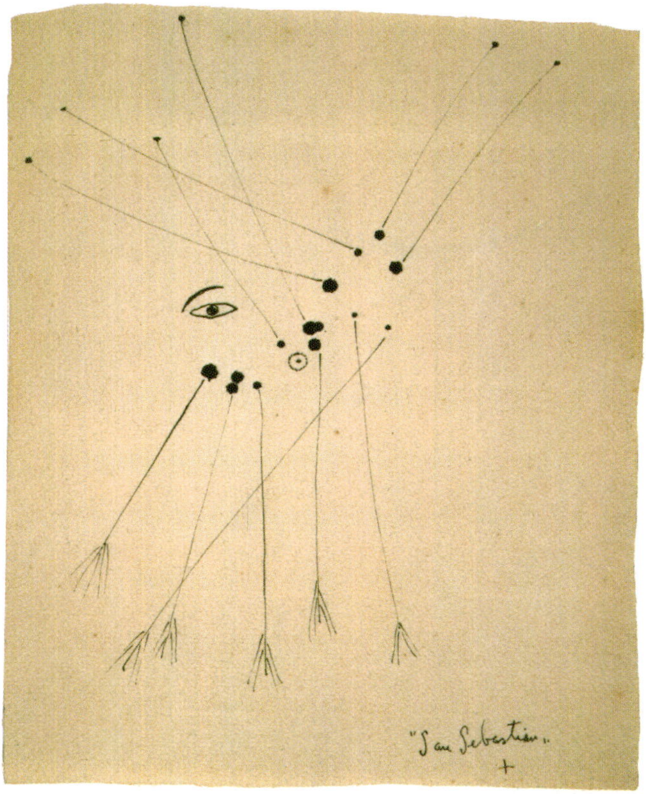

Federico García Lorca, *San Sebastián*, 1927. India ink on a piece of laid paper cut from a larger sheet. 155 x 125 mm. (Hernández no. 130). Private collection, Madrid. Sent to Sebastià Gasch in a letter of 1927, in which Lorca comments on a series of drawings: "You're right in all you said. But my state is not one of *perpetual dream*. I expressed myself badly. I have *circled around* dream on some days, but without ever falling fully into it, and always keeping a safety-rope of laughter and a firm wooden scaffold. I never venture into terrain that does not belong to man, because I turn back right away, and almost always *rip up* the product of my voyage. When I do something purely abstract, it aways has (I think) a passport of smiles and a rather human equilibrium. These last few drawings I've done have taken a good deal of work at elaboration. I abandoned my hand to the virgin earth, and my hand - together with my heart- brought me the mirculous elements. I was discovering them and noting them down. I cast my hand out again and thus, with many elements, I chose the characteristic elements of the matter at hand or the most beautiful and inexplicable, and I composed my drawing. Thus I composed the *Sevilian Bullfighter* [Hernández no. 132], the *Siren*, the *Saint Sebastian* and almost all of the ones that have a little cross" (*EC* 518-19). Months later, Lorca wrote to Dalí, comparing their respective visions of the saint: "His arrows are made of steel and the difference between you and me is that you see them fastened in him— fixed, stout, short arrows *which never grow rusty*—and I see them as long ones, at the very moment they have wounded him."

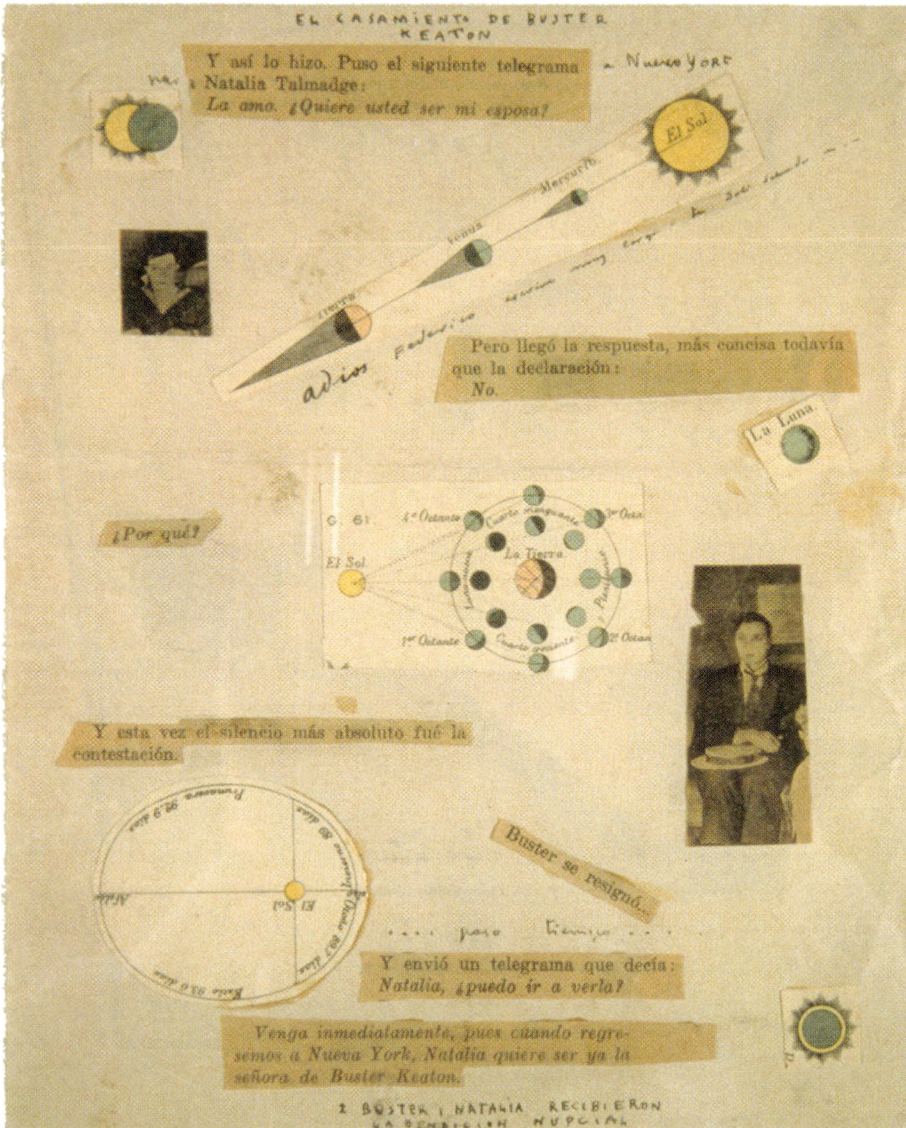

Salvador Dalí, *The Marriage of Buster Keaton*, collage. Sent to Lorca in a letter of February or March 1926. A sheet which accompanies this one reads: "Sainte Vierge Marie, Rene du ciel. Priez pour nous!" (Holy Virgin Mary, Queen of Heaven, pray for us!"). The maps show Shanghai, Granada, Greece, and the Catalan

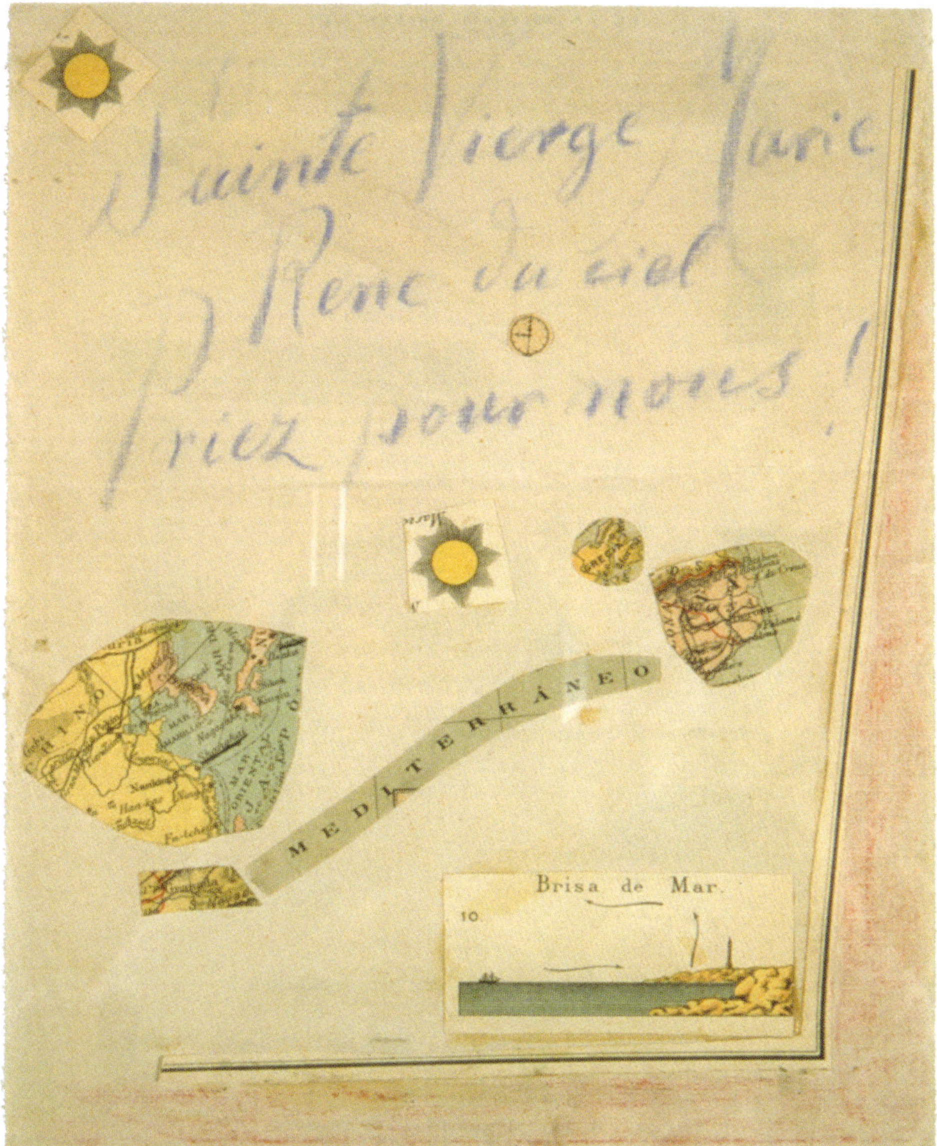

Coast, and the arrow between them suggests the common culture of what Dalí and Lorca liked to call *"our* Mediterranean" (see letter 6). "The Mediterranean is one and indivisible," Lorca wrote to Dalí's sister (letter 14), alluding to an aesthetic common to Granada and Cataluña.

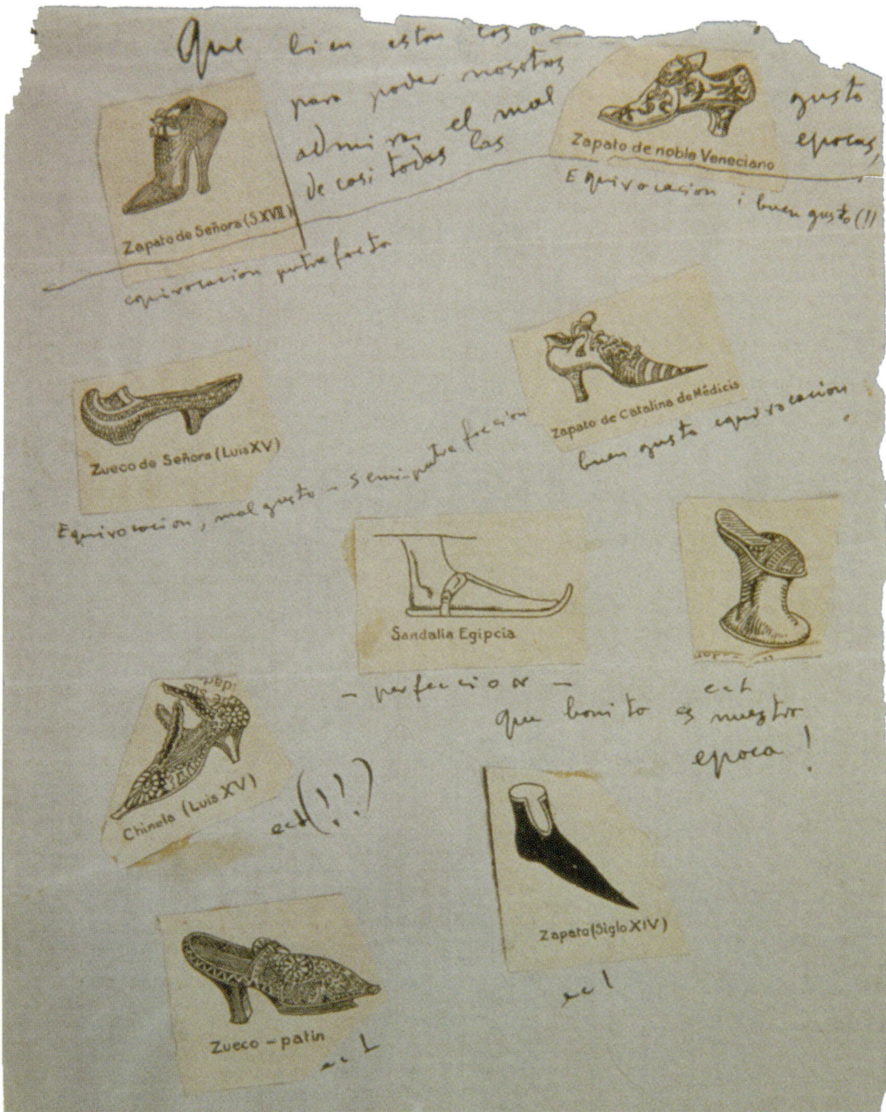

Salvador Dalí, *Shoe Collage*, collage, 1926, made during a period when Dalí greatly admired—and wrote about—the beauty of mass-produced objects and complained about unnecessary ornamentation. The hand-written captions read : "How nicely [these drawings] permit us to admire the bad taste of almost every period." Each of the shoes bears a caption. XVIIth century woman's shoe: "Mistake, putrefaction." Shoe of Venetian noble: "Mistake, good taste!!" Woman's clogs (Louis XV): "Mistake, bad taste—semiputrefaction." Catalina de Médicis Shoe: "Good taste, mistake." Egyptian sandal: "Perfection. How lovely is our epoch!" The others are marked "etc."

(1)

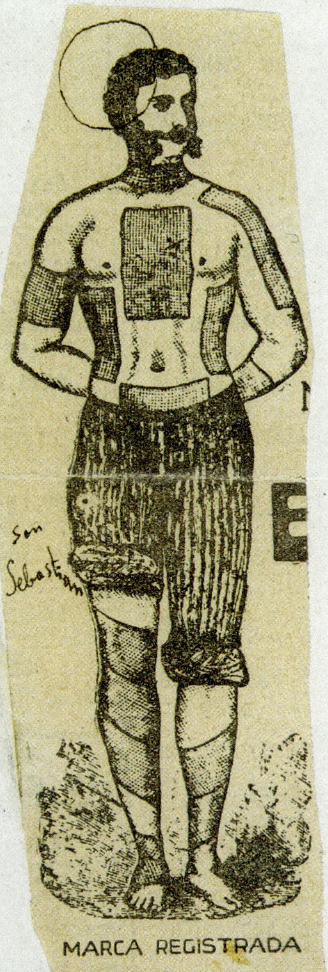

Querido Federico: He pasado casi un mes en Barcelona con motivo de mi exposición, ahora vuelvo a estar en Figueras maravillosamente con un nuevo estok de discos para el fonografo y infinitas cosas antiguas y de hoy para leer. ~~en Barcelona~~

Y con muchos modros en la punta de los dedos no en la cabeza.

Como ves te invito, a un nuevo tipo de San Sevastian que consiste en la pura transmutacion de la Flecha por el Lenguado – El principio de la elegancia es el que hacia a Sevastian deliciosamente agonizar, en este es un sentido anti-elegante que lo lleva coviardemente a convalecer; pero tenia que ser asi, yo te lo propongo para una temporada, quizas con el nuevo convoio encontraremos otro dia, la verdadera temperatura fria ~~de el frio~~ de las flechas

Salvador Dalí, *San Sebastián*. Dalí has clipped from a newspaper, and pasted to one of his letters to Lorca, the figure from a newspaper advertisement for "Sor Virginia" poultices, converting it into an image of Saint Sebastian. The same figure reappears in 1934 on the invitation to his exhibition at the Julien Levy Gallery, New York.

Federico García Lorca, *PORTRAIT OF DALI*. Colored pencils and ink, measurements unknown, c. 1925. The words on Dalí's palette are BLEU / AZUL / VERDE / NEGRO / GRIS [bleu, blue, green, black, grey]. Romero Gómez family, Granada. (Hernández no. 82)

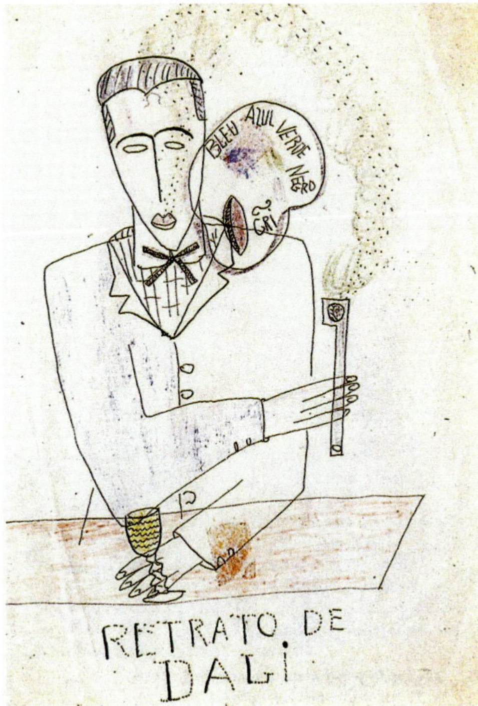

Federico García Lorca, *SLAVDOR ADIL (Peintre)*, colored pencils and ink on paper, 160 x 140 mm. with dedication (crossed out): "For my friend Ana María Dalí. Portrait of her Brother." Sent to Dalí's sister in a letter of September, 1925 (letter 8.) Lorca has written on the palette: AZUL / BLEU / ROUGE / SRGI [=gris]: BLUE, BLEU, ROUGE, GRAY. Casa-Museo Federico García Lorca, Granada. (Hernández no. 83)

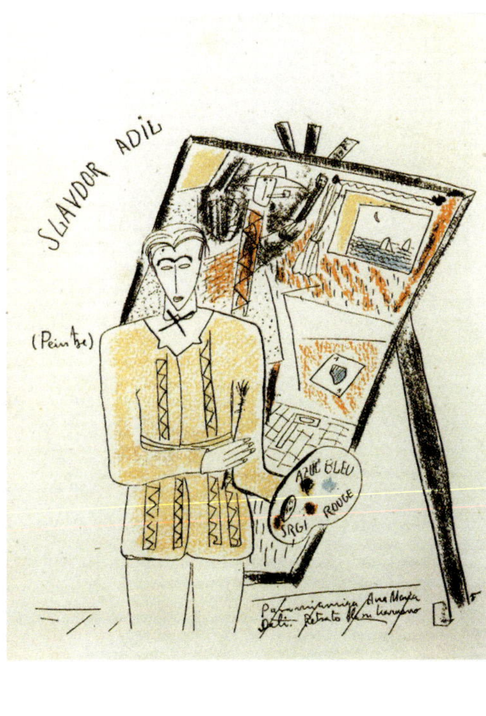

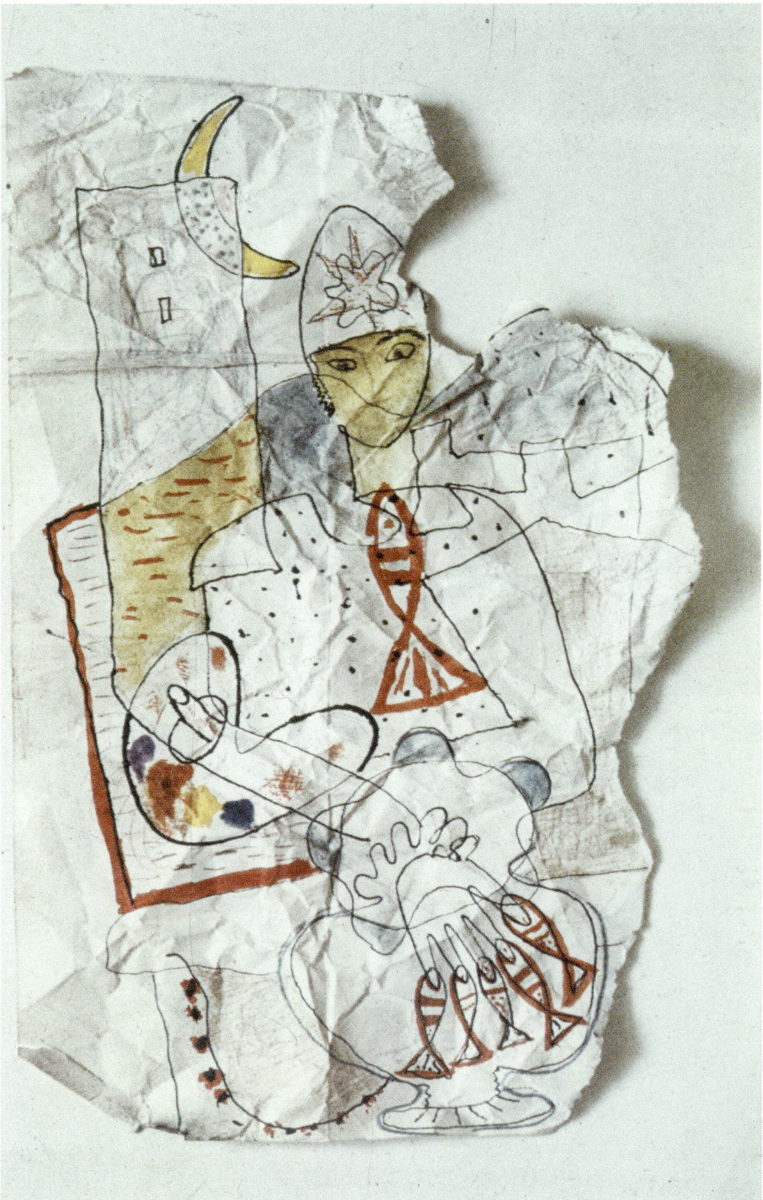

Federico García Lorca, *Portrait of Dalí,* c. 1927. Dimensions unknown (Hernández 116). Given by Lorca to Dalí and now in the Fundació Gala-Salvador Dalí. The drawing probably dates from the period of Dalí's essay *The Liberation of the Fingers:* "Often my own thumb gave me a sudden turn, despite my being used to seeing it isolated, sticking out of the hole in my palette like something disturbing and unusual..." (*Collected Writings*, ed. Finkelstein, p. 101).

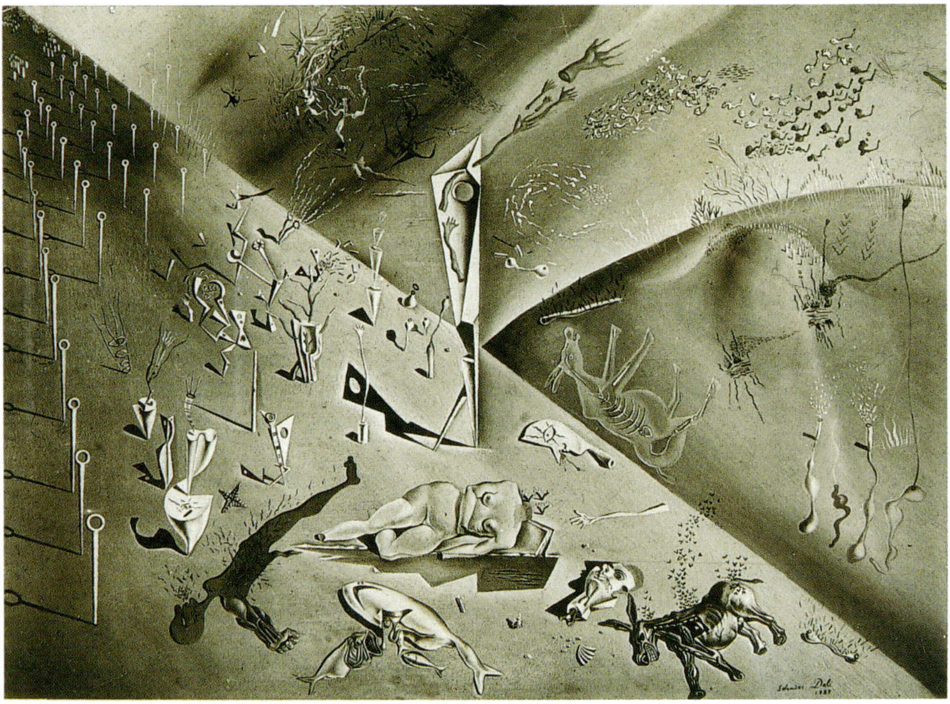

Salvador Dalí, *Honey is Sweeter than Blood,* 1927. Oil on canvas. Dimensions and location unknown. From a photo sent to Lorca by Dalí, in the Fundación Federico García Lorca.

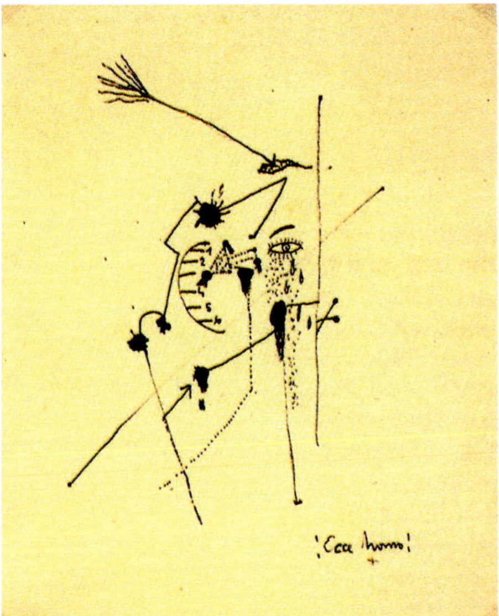

Federico García Lorca, *Ecce Homo!*, india ink on paper, 155 x 125 mm, c. 1927. Private collection, Madrid. Sent by Lorca to Sebastià Gasch. (Hernández no. 138)

33. SD to FGL

[Cadaqués, undated]

[...] You are a Christian whirlwind and you need my paganism. This past season in Madrid you surrendered to what you never should have. I'll go to get you to give you the sea cure. It will be winter and we will light a fire. The poor beasts will be freezing to death. You will remember that you are the inventor of marvelous things and we will live together with a camera [...]

34. FGL to Anna María Dalí

[Granada, mid-August 1927]

Dear Anna María:

I've been in Granada for a couple of days and all day long I have to describe you to my sisters, who are always asking about you.

I had such a wonderful time in Cadaqués that it all seems a wonderful dream. Above all, waking up and finding *that*—the thing one sees from the window. My good angels were the precious holy man Salvador de Horta and [José] Puig Pujades, who gave me that gift. I can remember the smallest little details about my stay in your house. And I fall to my knees and beg your pardon if I did anything to bother you, for example, my *serious* throat ailment, which put you to so much trouble.

The doctor here has seen me and says it's a bit of pharyngitis, and that it is unimportant, though a bother—the same thing Enriquet had told me. I'm now in the Huerta de San Vicente, near Granada, and in a couple of days we're going to the sierra of Lanjarón and afterwards to Málaga to finish out the summer. I feel good. The house is big, surrounded by water and corpulent trees but *this is not the truth*. Here there is an incredible amount of *historical melancholy* which makes me remember that just, neutral atmosphere of your terrace, where Lidia sometimes lets out a stream of strong pepper so that everyone can be more aware of the visible grace of the air! I've gotten *L'Amic de les Arts* and have seen your brother's prodigious poem. Here in Granada we've translated it and it has deeply impressed everyone, especially my brother, who *wasn't expecting such a thing,* despite all I've told him. It's simply a new sort of prose, full of unsuspected relationships and the most subtle points of view.

Now, from here, it acquires a charm and a truly intelligent light that only doubles my admiration.

I have begun to work—on things that are really bad, naturally, but which amuse me and enliven the emphatic monotony that surrounds me. I hope you will write and send me news of all that goes on in Cadaqués, and how the sea is doing, and how are the Marías, Eduardo and little Margarita. Say hello to Rosita for me, with great affection, and as for you, please sing "Once in Choralindo" in my honor.

Don't forget to feed the Geese!

Say hello to Raimunda.

Goodbye, Anna Maric. The little bear has sent me a postcard with something about [Eduardo] Marquina and telling me you've almost forgotten me, but that *he* can't forget me because of the admiration he feels and how well I've treated him.

In a couple of days I'll send you a cane. I beg you to tell him.

Say hello to your brother, the Little Fool (you know? Naw?)

Remember me to your father and for you all the affection that this friend, this *amic,* can possibly offer.

FEDERICO

Write me and tell me what your brother is painting.

Send me the photos, won't you?

35. FGL to Anna María Dalí

[Granada, mid-September 1927]

Dear friend Ana Patera y Seachera de Cuca,

I'm in bed, where I've received your lovely photos and pretty sketches.

I have been very ill for the past four days with a fever of 102. I've had a bad attack of food poisoning, and thank God haven't died, but I really felt bad. Today, sitting up in bed, I'm writing to give you my very best, prettiest and nicest thanks, and to send you this photograph of my sisters. They don't look all that great, but they're recognizable. They signed them for you.

I can't write any more because I feel dizzy. I'm only doing this as a token of affection and of the very best friendship.

I'll answer Mr. Marquina the Little Bear very soon.

He's so cute, so cute.

Goodbye. Until I get better. I'll write then. Much affection from your friend

FEDERICO

36. SD to FGL

[Cadaqués, September 1928]

Dear Federico,

I have read your book [*The Gypsy Ballads*] calmly and can't help commenting on a few things. Naturally, I can't share the opinions of the great putrescent pigs who have already spoken about it—Andrenio, etc. etc. But I believe my opinions about poetry are firmer every day, and that what I say will be of some interest.

I. To me, the best part of the book is the *last* part, the martyrdom of St. Eulalia, chunks of incest—*murmur of a hidden rose*—; these things go beyond mere local color and are less anecdotal than others. *The worst part,* I think, is the one about the fellow who *carries her down to the river.* Wit and humor produced by a state of mind based on appreciation, sentimentally deformed by *anachronism.* The one about the little saint in his alcove (Saint Gabriel) is, to me, today—when all I can bear in any production is the *rage* of its creator—a sort of immorality; this is what the French have used, *esprit,* the revolting and inadmissible Cocteau, etc., and we have all been contaminated by it.

II. Your present poetry belongs completely to the *traditional.* In it, I see the *hugest poetic substance that ever was,* but completely bound to the norms of the old poetry, which is no longer capable of moving us or satisfying our present-day desires. Your poetry is tied hands and feet to the old poetry. You probably think some of your images very bold, but I can assure you that your poetry moves within the *illustration* of the commonest and most conformist of commonplaces. For I'm convinced that in poetry our efforts only make sense when they lead us to evade the ideas our intelligence has forged artificially, and give things their exact, real sense.

In reality, there is no relation at all between two dancers and a honeycomb, unless it be the relation that exists between Saturn and the little cockroach that sleeps in its chrysalis, or unless there is *no difference* between the dancing couple and the honeycomb.

The minute-hands of a clock (never mind my examples, I'm not exactly looking for poetic ones) begin to have real value at the moment they stop pointing out the hours and, losing their *circular* rhythm and the arbitrary role our intelligence has subjected them to (pointing out the hours), they *evade* the clock entirely and occupy the place that would correspond to the sex organs of little bread crumbs.

You move within accepted, anti-poetic notions—you talk about a rider, and you suppose that he's riding a horse, and that the horse is galloping, *and this is already too much,* for in *reality* it would be better for you to ask whether it is really the rider who is on the horse; if the reins aren't really an organic extension of his very hands; if, in reality, the little hairs on the rider's balls aren't much faster than the horse; and if the horse isn't something immobile, fastened to the earth by vigorous roots. Etc. etc. Well, just *think* what it is to leap—as you do—to the concept of a Civil Guard. Poetically, the Civil Guard has no real existence... Unless it be as a joyful, handsome, living, shining silhouette, given his conditions and qualities and the little pointy things that come out of him and his little belts, which are a visceral part of his uniform, etc. etc.

And *you*, rottenly, [create] the Civil Guard, and what does he *do?* Such and such, and such... irreality, irreality, anti-poetry, the formation of arbitrary notions about things. We must leave things *free of* the conventional ideas to which intelligence has subjugated them. At that moment those handsome little things will begin to act in accordance with their real, *consubstantial* manner of being. Let the things themselves decide where their shadows fall! And perhaps what we thought would cast a thick shadow casts none at all, etc. etc. Ugly? Beautiful? Words that have lost their meaning. Horror... that's something else. That's what we get, far from all *style*, from a poetic knowledge of reality, since lyricism is only possible within the more or less approximate notions our intelligence can perceive about reality.

There will be an article devoted to you in the *Gaceta [Literaria]* in which I talk about these things, and about the importance of the strictly objective datum, obtained anti-artistically by a rigorous analytical method. But enough! Every day I am less able to write things like this in letters, and more capable of writing long, substantive articles, full of ideas.

Federiquito, in your book, which I've carried off to read in the mineral places around here, I have seen you, the little beastling that you are, an erotic beastling with your sex and the *little eyes of your body*, and your hair, and your fear of death and your desire to *let the gentleman know* when you die, and your mysterious spirit, made from foolish little enigmas in strict horoscopic correspondence, and the strict horoscopic correspondence between your thumb and your dick, with the moisture of the lakes of saliva of certain species of *hairy planets*. I love you for what your book reveals you to be, which is just the opposite of the reality the putrified of this world have made up about you—the dusky gypsy with black hair, childish heart, etc. etc., that whole decorative, non-existent *Nestorian* Lorca who could only have been invented by artistic swine who are far from little fish and bears and from the soft, hard, and liquid silhouettes that surround us.

I love and admire you. You, a beast with your little fingernail—you who sometimes surrender more than half of your body to death, or death comes up your arm, from fingernails to shoulder, in a sterile effort. I have drunk death from your shoulder at those moments when you were absent from your own great arms, which were nothing but two slipcovers with flounces from the useless, unconscious tapestries at the Residencia. I admire the Flounder-Tongue I see in your book, the fat flounder who will someday be unafraid to shit on the Salinases of this world and will abandon rhyme and all the other stuff that swine associate with art, and who will do things that are more fun and revolting and curly and poetic than any poet has ever done.

Goodbye, I *believe* in your inspiration, in your *sweat,* in your astronomical fatality.

This winter I invite you to leap with me into the void. I've already been there for days, and have never had such security, and I now know something about *Statuary* and about *real* clarity, far from any aesthetic.

A big hug,

DALÍ

Surrealism is only *one means* of Evasion.

It is the Evasion itself that matters.

I have my manners in the margin of surrealism, but that is something living. As you can see, I speak differently now, and have the joy of thinking very differently than I did last summer (how refined I am, no?)

37. FGL to SD

[Granada, summer 1930]

Salvador, dear friend:

We haven't seen each other in ages and I would love to speak to you; in fact, I *need* to speak to you.

I've lived stupendously well in New York for a year, and now it's as if I didn't know you, and didn't know what to tell you, but it goes something like this. In January I'll have a lot of money and want to invite you to return to New York with me. You could spend six months there and then go back to Paris, or travel with me to Moscow.

I'm going to have an exhibition in New York, where I have a gallery and an enormous number of idiotic friends, fag millionaires and ladies who buy *new* paintings and who could make the winter very pleasant for us. You know how charming I am as a person and I believe that would be useful to you and that your marvelous spirit would see unheard-of things in that city, which is totally new and opposite in form and in dream to the renovated but rotten romanticism of Paris.

I'm dying to see your things. Send me photographs and tell me what you've done.

I have worked hard, and joyfully.

I want you to know my new stuff and the little film I've made with a black poet in New York which will be premiered when I go back there in an admirable theater on Eighth Street where they put on all the productions of the Russians and Germans.

I want to speak to you. I've been cut off for too long from your friendship.

Tell me what you're thinking. Write me a long letter.

Goodbye. Always yours,

FEDERICO

Whenever I break the chain of stupidity, whenever I climb into bed I feel stronger than ever and more of a poet than anyone.

Your house: Acera del Casino, 31.

I got a huge kick out of the fraud you were trying to perpetrate on my family, and it is a shame they didn't send you the money. I found out late, when they sent me the letter. If I had gotten it first, I would have wired you that little bit of money.

Write me!

38. SD to FGL

[Cadaqués, 12-15 April, 1934]

Dear Lorquito:

I am sure that it would be *fun* to see each other again, wouldn't you like to? You've been to Barcelona, what a shame you didn't come to Cadaqués where I'm spending a few months, after the 2nd of May I'm going to Paris for a month.

I'm working on a great opera project based on important people. Sacher-Masoch, Ludwig II of Bavaria, Bogen, etc. I think that together we could really do something. If you could come we could reach a better understanding about lots of things. Gala is terribly curious to meet you.

Remember when "the pure will fall"? All this jives very well with the sextuobsession of spectral and super-refined anachronism. Read my article in numbers 3 and 4 of *Minotaure*. There is also an article by Eluard about postcards which you'll like, and a *theoretical mise au point* by Breton on communications. It's very very important. Don't forget to answer right away. Your Buddho

SALVADOR DALÍ

39. SD to FGL

[1936]

Dear Federiquito:

What a shame you didn't come to see us in Paris, what a great time we would've had. We have to do things together again. *Yerma* is something full of the *darkest,* most surrealist ideas. We are spending two months in Port-Lligat, taking the cure of Objectivity and analysis and eating all those extravagant things that NO ONE knows about, which are those stuffed chickpeas so superfine and smooth that they are delightful to look at and they are the very Eleusian mysteries, as far as food goes. *Tell me what you're doing and what you're thinking of doing.* We will always be glad to see you approaching our house. You remember that delirious structure of flesh and blood (can hardly believe it) who titled himself MAX Aub?

Gala sends you her affection, and I send you a big hug.

SALVADOR DALÍ

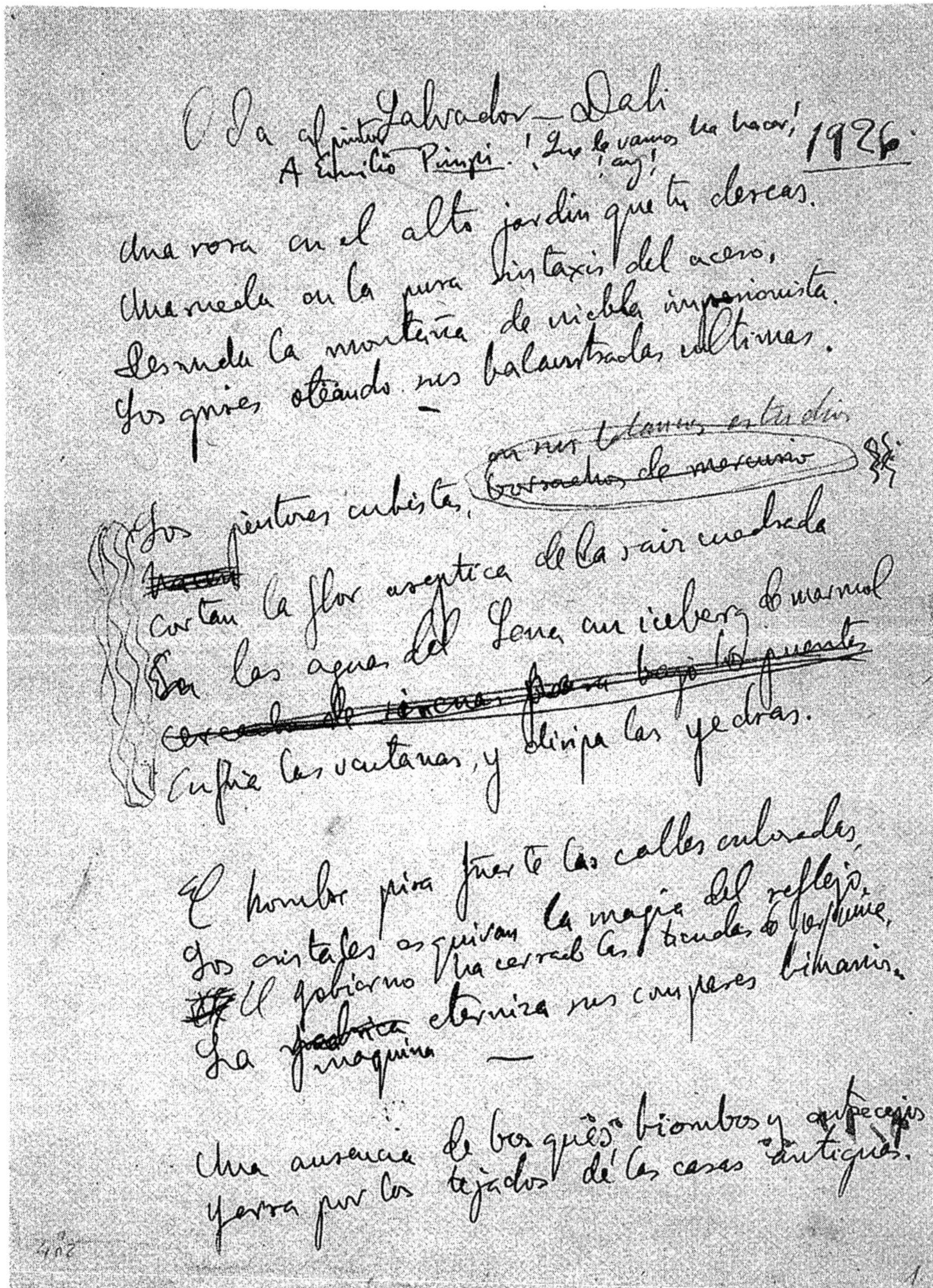

Oda al pintor Salvador Dalí
A Estrellita Pimpi. ¡Qué le vamos ha hacer! ¡ay!
1926.

Una rosa en el alto jardín que tú deseas.
Una rueda en la pura sintaxis del acero.
Desnuda la montaña de niebla impresionista.
Los grises oteando sus balaustradas últimas.

Los pintores cubistas, en sus blancos estudios
cortan la flor aséptica de la raíz cuadrada
En las aguas del Sena un iceberg de mármol
enfría las ventanas, y disipa las yedras.

El hombre pisa fuerte las calles enlosadas,
Los cristales esquivan la magia del reflejo.
El Gobierno ha cerrado las tiendas de perfume.
La máquina eterniza sus compases binarios.

Una ausencia de bosques, biombos y entrecejos
yerra por los tejados de las casas antiguas.

Federico Garcia Lorca, manuscript (rough draft) of "Ode to Salvador Dali," 1925.

Oda a Salvador Dalí
Ode to Salvador Dalí

Federico García Lorca

Oda a Salvador Dalí

Una rosa en el alto jardín que tú deseas.
Una rueda en la pura sintaxis del acero.
Desnuda la montaña de niebla impresionista.
Los grises oteando sus balaustradas últimas.

Los pintores modernos en sus blancos estudios,
cortan la flor aséptica de la raíz cuadrada.
En las aguas del Sena un *ice-berg* de mármol
enfría las ventanas y disipa las yedras.

El hombre pisa fuerte las calles enlosadas.
Los cristales esquivan la magia del reflejo.
El Gobierno ha cerrado las tiendas de perfume.
La máquina eterniza sus compases binarios.

Una ausencia de bosques, biombos y entrecejos
yerra por los tejados de las casas antiguas.
El aire pulimenta su prisma sobre el mar
y el horizonte sube como un gran acueducto.

Marineros que ignoran el vino y la penumbra
decapitan sirenas en los mares de plomo.
La Noche, negra estatua de la prudencia, tiene
el espejo redondo de la luna en su mano.

Ode to Salvador Dalí

A rose in the high garden of your desire.
A wheel in the pure syntax of steel.
The mountain stripped of Impressionist mist.
The grays keeping watch over their final balustrades.

In their white studios, modern painters
clip the square root's hygienic flower.
In the waters of the Seine a marble iceberg
chills windows and scatters ivy.

Man treads firmly on the cobblestone streets.
Glass shies from the magic of reflections.
The government has closed the perfume stores.
The machine perpetuates its binary rhythms.

An absence of forests, dressing screens and wrinkled brows
wanders over the roofs of the old houses.
The air polishes its prism over the sea
and the horizon rises like a great aqueduct.

Sailors who know nothing of wine and penumbra
decapitate sirens on leaden seas.
Night, black statue of prudence,
holds the round mirror of the moon.

Un deseo de formas y límites nos gana.
Viene el hombre que mira con el metro amarillo.
Venus es una blanca naturaleza muerta
y los coleccionistas de mariposas huyen.

*

Cadaqués, en el fiel del agua y la colina,
eleva escalinatas y oculta caracolas.
Las flautas de madera pacifican el aire.
Un viejo dios silvestre da frutas a los niños.

Sus pescadores duermen, sin ensueño, en la arena.
En alta mar les sirve de brújula una rosa.
El horizonte virgen de pañuelos heridos
junta los grandes vidrios del pez y de la luna.

Una dura corona de blancos bergantines
ciñe frentes amargas y cabellos de arena.
Las sirenas convencen, pero no sugestionan,
y salen si mostramos un vaso de agua dulce.

*

¡Oh Salvador Dalí, de voz aceitunada!
No elogio tu imperfecto pincel adolescente
ni tu color que ronda la color de tu tiempo,
pero alabo tus ansias de eterno limitado.

A desire for forms and limits overtakes us.
Here comes the man who looks with his yellow ruler.
Venus is a white still life
and the butterfly collectors flee.

*

Cadaqués, at the fulcrum of hill and water,
hides conch shells and raises flights of stairs.
Wooden flutes pacify the air.
An old sylvan god hands out fruit to children.

Her fishermen sleep dreamlessly on the sand.
On the high seas a rose serves them as compass.
The horizon, virgin of wounded handkerchiefs,
joins the huge glasses of the fish and the moon.

A hard crown of white brigantines
encircles bitter brows and hair of sand.
The sirens convince, but do not compel,
and they come out when offered a glass of water.

*

Oh Salvador Dalí with your olive-colored voice!
I do not praise your imperfect adolescent brush
or your color, which skirts the color of your age,
but I praise your yearning for eternity with limits.

Alma higiénica, vives sobre mármoles nuevos.
Huyes la oscura selva de formas increíbles.
Tu fantasía llega donde llegan tus manos,
y gozas el soneto del mar en tu ventana.

El mundo tiene sordas penumbras y desorden
en los primeros términos que el humano frecuenta.
Pero ya las estrellas ocultando paisajes
señalan el esquema perfecto de sus órbitas.

La corriente del tiempo se remansa y ordena
en las formas numéricas de un siglo y otro siglo.
Y la muerte vencida se refugia temblando
en el círculo estrecho del minuto presente.

Al coger tu paleta, con un tiro en un ala,
pides la luz que anima la copa del olivo.
Ancha luz de Minerva, constructora de andamios,
donde no cabe el sueño ni su flora inexacta.

Pides la luz antigua que se queda en la frente,
sin bajar a la boca ni al corazón del hombre.
Luz que temen las vides entrañables de Baco
y la fuerza sin orden que lleva el agua curva.

Hygienic soul, you live on new marbles,
fleeing the dark thicket of incredible forms.
Your fantasy reaches as far as your hands
and you enjoy the sonnet of the sea in your window.

The world has dumb half-shadow and disorder
in the foreground inhabited by man.
But the stars, hiding landscapes,
have come to reveal the perfect scheme of their orbits.

Time's current pools up and orders itself
in the numerical forms of one century and another.
And conquered Death takes trembling refuge
in the narrow circle of the present minute.

When you pick up your palette, a bullet hole in its wing,
you ask for the light that enlivens the olive tree:
ample light of Minerva, builder of scaffolds,
where there is no room for dream or her inexact flora.

You ask for the ancient light that stays on the brow,
without descending to man's heart or mouth.
Light feared by the beloved vines of Bacchus
and the chaotic force of curving water.

Haces bien en poner banderines de aviso
en el límite oscuro que relumbra de noche.
Como pintor no quieres que te ablande la forma
el algodón cambiante de una nube imprevista.

El pez en la pecera y el pájaro en la jaula.
No quieres inventarlos en el mar o en el viento.
Estilizas o copias después de haber mirado
con honestas pupilas sus cuerpecillos ágiles.

Amas una materia definida y exacta
donde el hongo no pueda poner su campamento.
Amas la arquitectura que construye en lo ausente
y admites la bandera como una simple broma.

Dice el compás de acero su corto verso elástico.
Desconocidas islas desmiente ya la esfera.
Dice la línea recta su vertical esfuerzo
y los sabios cristales cantan sus geometrías.

*

Pero también la rosa del jardín donde vives.
¡Siempre la rosa, siempre, norte y sur de nosotros!
Tranquila y concentrada como una estatua ciega,
ignorante de esfuerzos soterrados que causa.

You do well to nail *banderillas*
into the dark limit that shines with night.
As a painter you don't want your forms softened
by the shifting cotton of an unforeseen cloud.

The fish in its bowl, the bird in its cage:
You do not wish to invent them in sea or wind.
You stylize or copy after peering
with honest pupils at their agile little bodies.

You love the exact, well-defined matter
where the toadstool cannot pitch its camp
and the architecture that builds in the absent
and you consider the flag a simple joke.

The steel compass tells its short, elastic verse.
The sphere denies islands that are unknown.
The straight line tells of its vertical struggle
and wise crystals sing their geometries.

*

But also the rose in the garden where you live.
Always, always the rose. Our north and south!
Calm, concentrated, like a blind statue
oblivious to the hidden struggles it causes.

Rosa pura que limpia de artificios y croquis
y nos abre las alas tenues de la sonrisa.
(Mariposa clavada que medita su vuelo.)
Rosa del equilibrio sin dolores buscados.
¡Siempre la rosa!

*

¡Oh Salvador Dalí de voz aceitunada!
Digo lo que me dicen tu persona y tus cuadros.
No alabo tu imperfecto pincel adolescente,
pero canto la firme dirección de tus flechas.

Canto tu bello esfuerzo de luces catalanas,
tu amor a lo que tiene explicacióñ posible.
Canto tu corazón astronómico y tierno,
de baraja francesa y sin ninguna herida.

Canto el ansia de estatua que persigues sin tregua,
el miedo a la emoción que te aguarda en la calle.
Canto la sirenita de la mar que te canta
montada en bicicleta de corales y conchas.

Pero ante todo canto un común pensamiento
que nos une en las horas oscuras y doradas.
No es el Arte la luz que nos ciega los ojos.
Es primero el amor, la amistad o la esgrima.

Pure rose, clean of artifice and sketches
which opens on our lips the tenuous wings of a smile
(pinned butterfly meditating its flight.)
Rose of equilibrium, seeking no pains.
Always the rose!

*

Oh, Salvador Dalí with your olive-colored voice!
I say what your persons and your paintings tell me.
I do not praise your imperfect adolescent brush,
but sing the firm direction of your arrows.

I sing your sweet struggle of Catalan lights.
Your love of what can be explained.
I sing your tender, astronomical heart,
a deck of French cards that has never been wounded.

I sing your implacable longing for the statue,
your fear of the feeling that can ambush you in the street.
I sing the little sea siren who sings to you
from her bicycle of corals and conches.

But above all I sing the common thought
that joins us in both dark and golden hours.
The light that blinds our eyes is not Art,
but love, friendship, and fencing.

Es primero que el cuadro que paciente dibujas
el seno de Teresa, la de cutis insomne,
el apretado bucle de Matilde la ingrata,
nuestra amistad pintada como un juego de oca.

Huellas dactilográficas de sangre sobre el oro
rayen el corazón de Cataluña eterna.
Estrellas como puños sin halcón te relumbren,
mientras que tu pintura y tu vida florecen.

No mires la clepsidra con alas membranosas,
ni la dura guadaña de las alegorías.
Viste y desnuda siempre tu pincel en el aire
frente a la mar poblada con barcos y marinos.

It isn't the picture you draw so patiently,
but the breast of Teresa—she of sleepless flesh—
the tight wound curls of ungrateful Mathilde,
our friendship, painted bright as a game board.

May fingerprints of blood on gold
streak the heart of eternal Cataluña.
May stars like fists without a hawk illumine you
while your painting and your life blossom.

Pay no heed to the water clock with its membranous wings,
or the harsh scythe of the allegory.
Bathe and undress your brush in the air
before a sea of sailors and ships.

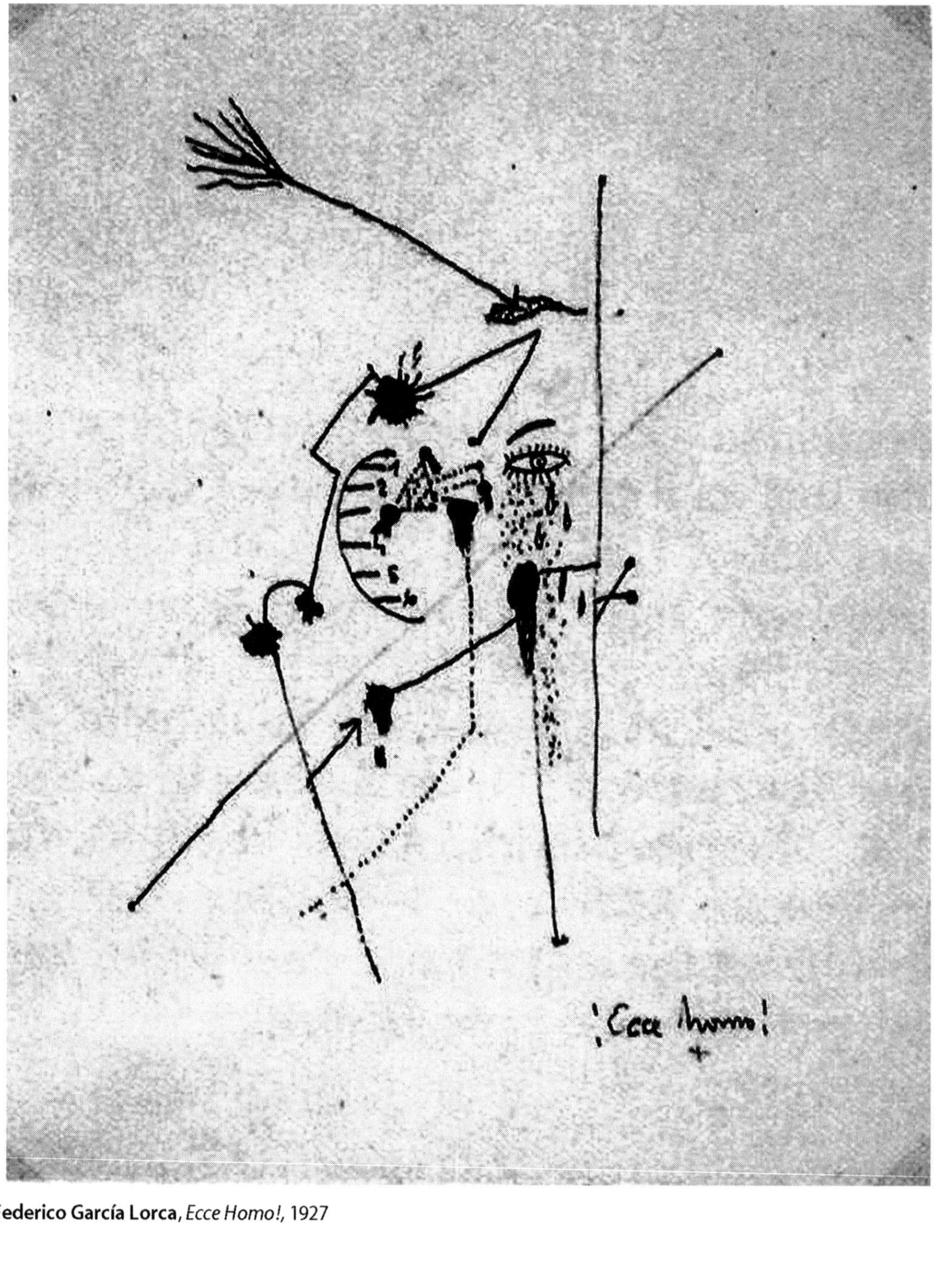

Federico García Lorca, *Ecce Homo!*, 1927

St. Lucy and St. Lazarus

Federico García Lorca

It was midnight when I got to the city, and the frost was dancing on one foot.

"A girl can be blonde or brunette, but she oughtn't to be blind," said the innkeeper to a man brutally dissected by a sash. The eyes of a mule dozing in the doorway threatened me like two jet-black fists.

"I want the very best room you have."

"There's only one."

"Let me see it."

The room had a mirror, and I, half a comb in my pocket.

"It's fine" (and I saw my "fine" in the green mirror).

The innkeeper shut the door. "It's fine," I said again, my back to the frozen little field of mercury. Downstairs the mule was panting. I mean that he opened the sunflower of his mouth.

There was nothing to do but climb into bed. And that I did. But I took the precaution of leaving the shutters open, for there is nothing lovelier than to catch and frame a star by surprise. Just one. Forget the rest.

Tonight I have an irregular, whimsical sky, and the stars huddle together or cover the windowpanes like postcards and portraits on a Japanese rug.

*

At dawn my gray suit returned to the humid air. The spring day was like a hand swooning onto a cushion. People came and went, up and down the street, some of them selling fruit and fish.

Not a single bird.

As I thrummed my rings on the iron of the window grate, I looked for the city on the map, and saw that it was asleep in yellow, amid rich little veins of water, far from the sea!

In the courtyard, the innkeeper and his wife were singing a duet of hawthorn and violet. Their dark voices bumped into the walls, scurrying about like moles, without finding the square outlet to the sky.

Before going out on my first walk, I went to greet them.

"Why did you say last night that a girl can be blonde or brunette but not blind?"

The innkeeper and his wife looked at each other in a strange way.

They looked at each other... mistakenly. Like the boy who lifts a soup spoon to his eyes rather than his mouth. And they broke into tears.

I didn't know what to say, and left in a hurry.

In the door I read this sign: ST. LUCY'S INN.

*

St. Lucy was a lovely maiden of Syracuse.

They paint her with two magnificent ox eyes on a tray.

She suffered martyrdom under Paschasian the consul, who had silver mustaches and howled like a mastiff.

Like all saints, she proposed and resolved delightful theorems of the sort that demolish the instruments of physicists.

In a public square she demonstrated, to the amazement of bystanders, that one thousand men and fifty yoks of oxen are no match for the luminous little dove of the Holy Spirit. Her huge body turned into compressed lead. Surely Our Lord, with his scepter and crown, was sitting on her waist.

St. Lucy was an adult woman, with a small bosom and opulent hips. Like all fierce women, she had huge, manly eyes with an unpleasant dark light. She died on a bed of flames.

*

The market was at its height, and the beach of day was full of conch shells and ripe tomatoes. Standing before the miraculous facade of the cathedral, I suddenly realized how St. Raymond Nonnatus was able to cross the sea from the Balearics to Barcelona mounted on his cape, and how the ancient Sun of China leaps furiously over musical towers made of dragon flesh.

People were drinking beer in the bars and doing their accounts in offices, and the + and = of the Jewish bank were struggling darkly, full of saltpeter and snuffed out tapers, with the holy sign of the cross. The main bell of the cathedral showered the city with little copper bells that sank into stupefied streetcars and the nervous necks of horses. I had forgotten my guidebook and binoculars, and began to look at the city the way one stares at the sea from the beach.

The streets were lined with optical shops. Huge terrible eyes like those of prehistoric sloths peered from every facade. Terrible eyes, well outside the almond orbit that makes human ones so intense. Eyes that tried to hide their monstrousness, imitating the innocuous blinking eyes of every Tom, Dick and Harry. Eyeglasses and tinted lenses were looking for the huge cut hand of the glove maker's shop, a poem in the air, which resounds and bleeds and gurgles like the head of John the Baptist.

The city's gaiety had subsided, like a schoolboy who has just failed his exams. Until a few hours earlier, it had been joyful, crowned with trills and lined with bulrushes, but now the sadness that slackens electrical lines and lifts the paving stones of courtyards had invaded the streets with its imperceptible murmur: the murmur one hears in the depths of a mirror. I broke into tears. For there's nothing more moving than the sadness that settles on joyful things. A sadness that has yet to jell, when a little joy is still coming through, and the glint of coins with holes in them.

Newly minted sadness of copybooks with brand names like "The Umbrella," "The Automobile," and "The Bicycle." Sadness of a fifteen-year-old issue of *Blanco y Negro*. Sadness of embroidered petticoats. Poignant sadness of the gramophone horn.

In optical shops, apprentices were polishing crystals of all sizes with chamois and tissue paper, like the rustle of a serpent.

In the cathedral they were celebrating a solemn novena to the human eyes of St. Lucy.

They were glorifying the exterior of things, the clean airy beauty of the skin, the charm of slender surfaces, and they were praying for help against the dark physiologies of the body, the central fire, and the funnels of night, raising, under the seedless dome of the cathedral, a sheet of pure crystal, riddled by fine gold spotlights. The world of grass waged war with the mineral world.

Fingernail against heart. A god of contours, transparency and surface. Afraid of the pulse, horrified of the spurt of blood, they were praying for the tranquility of agates and the shadowless nudity of the jellyfish.

When I entered the cathedral, they were singing the lamentation of the six-thousand diopters, which echoed through the three cupolas filled with rigging and movements and waves like three battles of Lepanto. The eyes of St. Lucy peered from their salver, with the cold pain of an animal just killed with a dagger to the neck.

Space and distance. Vertical and horizontal. Relationship between you and me. Eyes of St. Lucy! The veins in the foot soles slumbered in their rosy beds, calmed by the two stars that shine down on them from above. We leave our eyes on the surface like aquatic flowers and crouch behind them, while our palpitating physiology floats through a dark, dark world.

I knelt.

The precentors fired their shotguns from the choir loft.

Meanwhile, night had come. A dark brutal night, like the head of a mule with leather blinders.

The skeleton of an old fish hung in one of the exit doors. In another, the skeleton of a seraph, swaying gently in the cool oval breeze of the optical shops, which wafted in with apples and seashores.

It was time to eat, and I asked my way back to the inn.

"You're very far from it. Don't forget the cathedral is near the train station, and that the inn is to the South, below the river."

"I have more than enough time."

*

The train station was very close.

Behind it was a wide square, hard as three in the morning, representing the lame emotion dragged about by the waning moon.

Little by little the glasses in the optical shop returned to their little leather and nickel coffins, in a silence subtly linking fish, star and spectacles.

Those who have seen their eyeglasses in the moonlight or have left their opera glasses on the beach understand, as I do, this delicate harmony (fish, star, spectacles) which comes tumultuously together on a big white tablecloth, newly bathed in champagne.

I managed to compose as many as eight still lifes with the eyes of St. Lucy.

St. Lucy's eyes in the foreground, set off by clouds, with the air of someone who has just lost his birds.

St. Lucy's eyes on the ocean, in the sphere of the clock, on each side of the anvil, and in the huge newly-cut tree trunk.

They can be related to the desert, to large, intact surfaces, to a marble foot, a thermometer and an ox.

They cannot be joined to mountain, spindle, toad, or cottony materials. St. Lucy's eyes.

Far from any pulse, far from any sorrow. Permanent. Inactive. Unwavering. Watching all things take flight, wrapped in their difficult eternal temperature. Worthy of the tray that makes them real, rising up like the breasts of Venus before the ironic monocle used by an evil enemy.

*

I resumed my walk, springing along on my rubber soles.

I was crowned in a magnificent silence, surrounded everywhere by grand pianos.

In the darkness I could easily make out a sign made with electric light bulbs. ST. LAZARUS STATION.

*

St. Lazarus was very pale at birth and he smelled like a wet sheep. When they whipped him, little cubes of sugar came from his mouth. He could hear the slightest sounds. He once confessed to his mother that he could tell from their beating hearts how many people there were in the village.

He had a predilection for the strange silence that is towed about by fish, and whenever he went through an archway he shrank back in terror. After coming back to life he invented the coffin, the taper, magnesium lights, and railway stations. When he died he was hard and laminated like a loaf of silver. His soul came along behind him, deflowered by the other world, very annoyed, a reed in its hand.

*

The mail train had left at midnight.

I had to catch the express at two in the morning.

Entrances to cemeteries and train platforms.

Same air, same emptiness, same broken glass.

The rails fading into the distance, pulsing in their perspective like a theorem, outstretched and dead, like the arms of Christ on the cross.

Rigid apples of fear fell from the rooftops.

In a nearby tailor's shop, scissors were cutting endless pieces of white cloth.

Cloth to shroud everything, from the withered breast of the old lady to the weeny of the newborn child.

Another traveler was approaching. Just one.

He was wearing a white summer suit with mother of pearl buttons and a light overcoat of the same color. His big dull eyes were shining between his aquiline nose and newly cleaned hat.

His right hand was hard plaster, and a reed basket, full of hens eggs, dangled from his arm.

I wasn't able to tell him a thing.

He seemed distracted, as though waiting to be called. He warded off pallor with his Oriental beard, a beard that clothed him in mourning for his own death.

An utterly real mortal scheme monogrammed my tie in nickel.

That night was a holiday, and all Spain crowded to the railings to watch a black bull who looked sadly at the sky and bellowed every four minutes.

The traveler was in the country that best suited him, on a night that suited his yearning for perspective. He was waiting for daybreak to fly away in search of inexorable voices.

The Spanish night—night of red earth and iron nails—barbarous night with its breasts exposed, caught in a unique telescope—blessed the chilly traveler. He liked its unfathomable depths, and took pleasure in sinking his feet right down to its foundation of ash and hot sand.

The traveler strolled along the platform with the logic of a fish in water or a fly in the air. He walked to and fro, without noticing the long, sad parallels of those waiting for the train.

I felt great pity for him, for I knew he was awaiting a voice, and to wait for a voice is like sitting on the guillotine in the middle of the French Revolution.

Shot in the shoulder, unexpected telegram, surprise... until the wolf falls into the trap, it knows no fear. Silence, the heartbeat... these are pleasant things. But waiting for a surprise is like turning a fleeting instant into a huge purple balloon that swells and doesn't go away and fills the entire night.

The sound of an approaching train seemed as confused as a drubbing.

I picked up my suitcase and the man in the white suit looked in all directions.

And finally a clear voice, the stamen of an authoritarian loudspeaker, cried out from the depths of the station: "Lazarus! Lazarus! Lazarus!" And the traveler broke into a run, docile, full of unction, until he was lost in the last lamps.

The instant I heard the voice—"Lazarus! Lazarus! Lazarus!"—my mouth filled with fig marmalade.

*

I got home a few moments ago.

I wasn't surprised to find my suitcase empty. There were only some eyeglasses and a very white overcoat. The two themes of the trip. Pure and isolated. On the table, the eyeglasses reached extremes of concrete drawing and flat steadiness. The overcoat was swooning on a chair with an air of finality, at a distance that seemed rather inhuman, the sub-zero distance of a drowned fish. The eyeglasses were moving toward a geometrical theorem of exact demonstration, and the overcoat toward a sea full of shipwrecks and sudden green splendor.

Eyeglasses and overcoat on the table and on the chair. St. Lucy and St. Lazarus.

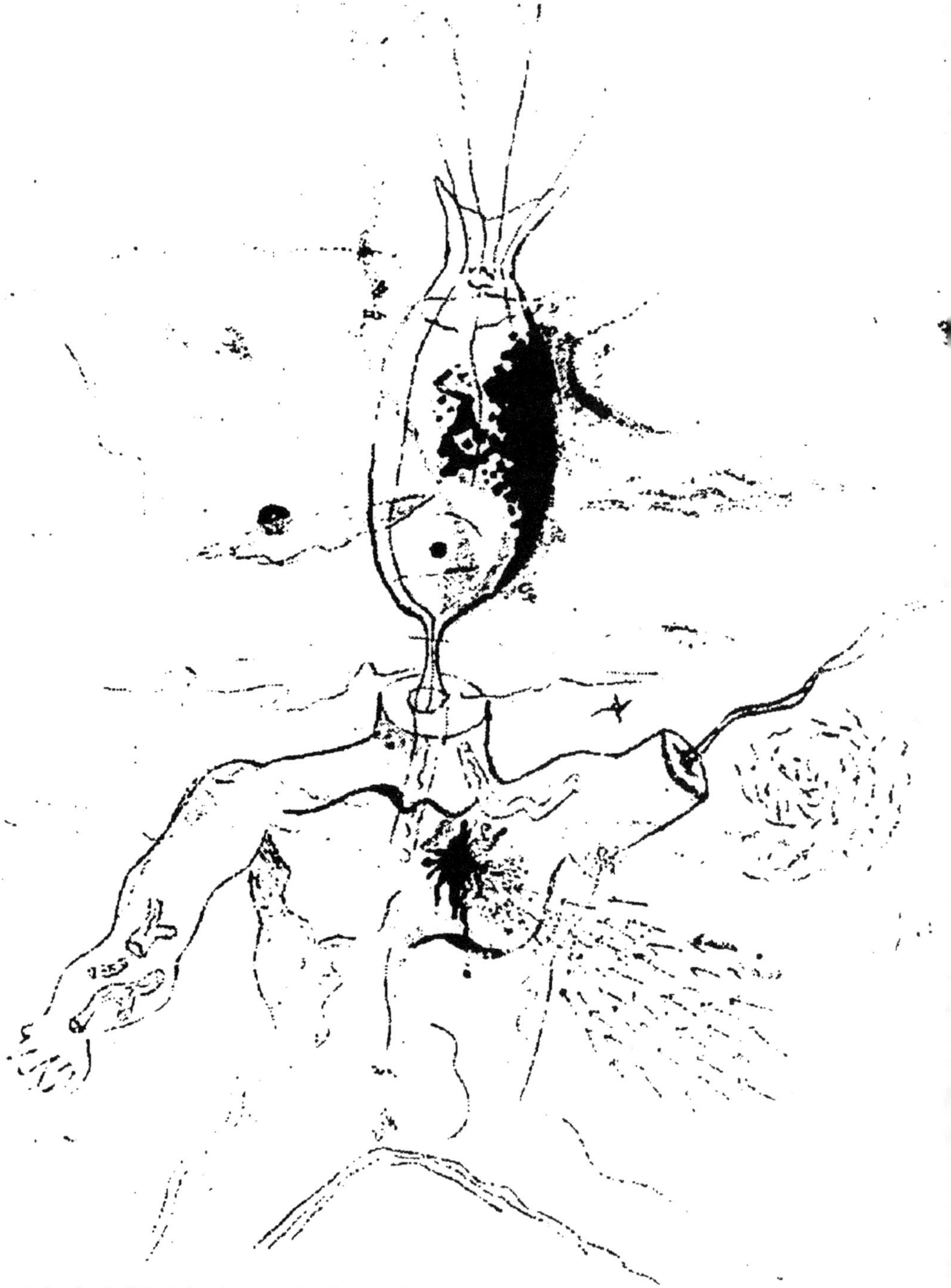

Salvador Dalí, *St. Sebastian,* 1927 (*See* letter 18)

St. Sebastian

Salvador Dalí

Irony

Heraclitus, in a fragment collected by Themistius, tells us that Nature likes to conceal herself. Alberto Savinio believes this concealment is motivated by modesty, for an apparently ethical reason, and that this modesty is born from Nature's relation to man. And he discovers in this the first cause of irony.

Enriquet, a fisherman from Cadaqués, told me much the same thing, in his own language, the day that he looked at a painting of mine of the sea and observed: "It's the same. But better in the picture, because in it one can count the waves."

In this preference, too, one could find the origin of irony, if Enriquet were able to go from physics to metaphysics.

Irony, I have said, is nakedness. It is the gymnast who hides behind St. Sebastian's pain. And it is also the pain itself, because it can be quantified.

Patience

There is a certain patience in Enriquet's rowing, which is a wise form of inaction. But there is also the patience that is a form of passion, the humble patience which ripens the pictures of Vermeer of Delft, which is the same sort of patience that brings fruit trees to maturity.

There is still another form: a form between inaction and passion, between the rowing of Enriquet and the painting of Van der Meer, which is a form of elegance. I am referring to the patience one finds in the exquisite death struggle of Saint Sebastian.

Description of the Figure of Saint Sebastian

I realized I was in Italy because of the black and white marble paving of the staircase. I went up it. At the end was Saint Sebastian, lashed to the old trunk of a cherry tree, his feet resting on a broken capital. The more I observed his figure, the more curious it seemed. But I had the impression I had known it all my life, and the aseptic morning light revealed the small details to me with such purity and clarity that it was impossible to feel perturbed.

The head of the saint was divided into two parts. One was formed by a material resembling that of a jellyfish, and held by a very thin hoop of nickle. The other was filled by half a face which reminded me of someone very familiar. From that hoop came a support of whitest plaster, which was like the figure's backbone. Each arrow was marked with its temperature and a little inscription, engraved on the steel, which said, "Invitation to a Coagulation of Blood." In certain parts of the body the veins appeared on the surface, with the intense blue of a storm by Patinir, tracing curves of a painful voluptuousness in the rosy coral of the flesh.

On reaching the shoulders of the saint, the direction of the breeze left an impression there, as though on a sensitive plate.

Trade Winds and Counter Trade Winds

On touching his knees, the thin air came to a stop. The martyr's halo was like rock crystal and in its hardened whisky there flowered a rough, bleeding starfish.

On the sand covered with shells and mica, the exact instruments of an unknown physics were projecting their explicative shadows, and offered their crystals and aluminiums to the disinfected light. Some letters drawn by Giorgio Morandi read: "Distilled apparatuses."

Sea Air

Every half minute came the smell of the sea, as constructed and anatomical as the pieces of a crab.

I breathed in. Nothing was mysterious any more. The smell of Saint Sebastian was a pure pretext for an aesthetics of objectivity. I breathed in again, and this time I closed my eyes, not out of mysticism, and not to see my inner self better—as one might say Platonically—but simply for the unique sensuality of the physiology of my eyelids.

Then I went on slowly reading the names and exact indications of the apparatuses. Each note was a point of departure for an entire series of intellectual delectations, and a new scale of precisions for unsuspected normalities.

Without any previous explication, I intuited the use of each apparatus and the joy of each of their sufficient exactitudes.

Heliometer for Deaf-Mutes

One of the apparatuses had this title: Heliometer for Deaf-Mutes. The name hinted at its relation to astronomy, and this was borne out by its construction. It was an instrument of high physical poetry formed by distances and by the relations of those distances and those relations were expressed geometrically in some parts and arithmetically in others. In the center, a simple gauge served to measure the agony of the saint. This mechanism was formed by a small dial of graduated plaster, in the center of which a scarlet drop of coagulated blood, trapped between two slides of glass, served as a sensible barometer of each new wound.

In the upper part of the heliometer was the magnifying glass of St. Sebastian. It was concave, convex and flat at the same time. Engraved on the silver mounting of those clear, precise crystals, one could read: "Invitations to Astronomy", and further down, in letters that seemed to stand out in relief: "Holy Objectivity." On a thick glass rod with numbers, one could read: "Measure of the apparent distances between pure esthetic values", and beside it, in a very thin, graduated test tube, this subtle notice: "Apparent distances and arithmetical measurements between pure sensual values." The test tube was half full of sea water.

In the heliometer of Saint Sebastian there was neither music nor voice, and in certain sections, it was blind. These blind points of the apparatus were those which corresponded to its sensible algebra, and those destined to make concrete even the most insubstantial, miraculous things.

Invitations to Astronomy

I brought my eye nearer to the magnifying glass, the product of a long numerical and intuitive distillation.

Each drop of water, a number. Each drop of blood, a geometry.

I looked. First, my eyelids caressed the wise surface made of calculations. Then I saw a succession of clear spectacles, perceived with such an ordering of measurements and proportions that each detail offered itself to me like a simple, eurythmic architectural organism.

On the deck of a white mailboat, a breastless girl was teaching sailors filled with the south wind to dance the black bottom. On other ocean liners, people dancing the Charleston and the blues saw Venus each morning in the bottom of their gin cocktails, at the hour of their pre-apéritifs.

There was nothing vague about all this, all was seen clearly, with the clarity of a magnifying glass. Whenever my eyes rested on a concrete detail, that detail was magnified as in a cinematographic close up, and revealed its highest plastic value.

I see the female polo player in the nickel-plated headlamp of an Isotta Fraschini. I do nothing but stare fixedly at her left eye, and this eye occupies my entire field of vision. That one eye, suddenly enlarged and like a visible sun, is an entire bottom and surface of an ocean, where all poetic suggestions are floating and all plastic possibilities are stabilized. Each eyelash is a new direction and a new stillness. The sticky, sweet mascara, in its microscopic enlargement, a precise sphere through which one can see the Virgin of Lourdes or the painting (1926) by Giorgio de

Chirico: *Evangelical Still Life.*

On reading the tender letters on the biscuit

Superior
Petit Beurre
Biscuit

my eyes filled with tears.

An arrow beneath it read: "Direction Chirico: towards the limits of a metaphysics."

The thin, thin line of blood is a still, wide map of the city. I don't want to continue until the life of the radiant leucocyte and the scarlet ramifications turn into a small blot, passing rapidly through all the phases of their diminution. The eyes rested again on the eye's primitive dimension, in the depths of the concave mirror of the headlamp, like an unheard-of organism in which the precise fish of the reflections swim in their teary, watery setting.

Before looking further, I lingered on the details of the saint. Saint Sebastian, free of symbolism, was a fact in his unique, simple presence. Only with so great an objectivity is it possible to calmly follow a stellar system. My heliometric vision continued. I was aware that I was perfectly within the anti-artistic and astronomical orbit of the Fox Newsreel.

Next came some entertainment—simple facts motivating our lyrical states.

The girl in the bar plays *Dinah* on her little phonograph while she prepares gin for the motorists, inventors of the subtle games of chance and of black superstition with the mathematics of their engines,

On the cement race track, blue Bugatti race cars, seen from an airplane, acquire the somnolent movements of hydroids which plunge down in a spiral to the bottom of the aquarium, with their parachutes opened.

The rhythm of Josephine Baker, in slow motion, coincides with the slower and purer growth of a flower in the cinematographic accelerator.

Again, cinematic breeze. White gloves and black piano keys of Tom Mix, pure as the last amorous interlacing of fish, crystals and stars of Marcoussis.

Adolphe Menjou in an anti-transcendental environment, gives a new dimension of tuxedos and ingenuousness (only enjoyable now from a cynical point of view).

Buster Keaton—how's *that* for Pure Poetry, Paul Valéry? Post-mechanistic avenues, Florida, Le Corbusier, Los Angeles, the pulchritude and eurythmics of the standardized object, aseptic, anti-artistic entertainments, concrete clarities, humble, alive, joyous, comforting, to oppose to art which is sublime, deliquescent, bitter, putrefied.

Laboratory, clinic.

The white clinic falls silent around the pure chromolithograph of a lung.

In the glass of the showcases, the chloroformed scalpel slumbers, like a sleeping beauty in the forest where nickel cannot combine with ripolin.

American magazines offer *Girls, Girls, Girls* to the eyes, and under the sun of Antibes, Man Ray obtains the clear *portrait* of a magnolia, which has a better effect on our flesh than the tactile creations of the Futurists.

Shop window of shoes in the Grand Hotel.

Tailors' dummies. Dummies resting in the electrical pomp of the store windows, with their neutral, mechanical sensualities and disturbing articulations. Live manikins, sweetly stupid, walking with an alternating rhythm, with hips and shoulders in opposite directions, pressing to their arteries the new, reinvented physiologies of clothes.

Putrefaction

The opposite side of the St. Sebastian's magnifying glass corresponded to putrefaction. Everything in it was anguish, obscurity and tenderness; tenderness because of the exquisite absence of spirit and naturalness.

Preceded by I know not what verses of Dante, I saw the entire world of the putrefied: blubbering transcendental artists, far from any sort of clarity, bearers of all germs, ignorant of the exactitude of the double graduated decimeter; families who buy objets d'art to put on their piano; the public works employee; the associate committee member; the professor of psychology. I did not want to continue. The thin mustache of an office worker moved me greatly. I felt in my heart all of its exquisite, subtle, Franciscan poetry. My lips smiled, though I felt like crying. I stretched out on the sand. The waves were coming to shore with the soft murmurs of Henri Rousseau's *Bohémienne endormie*.

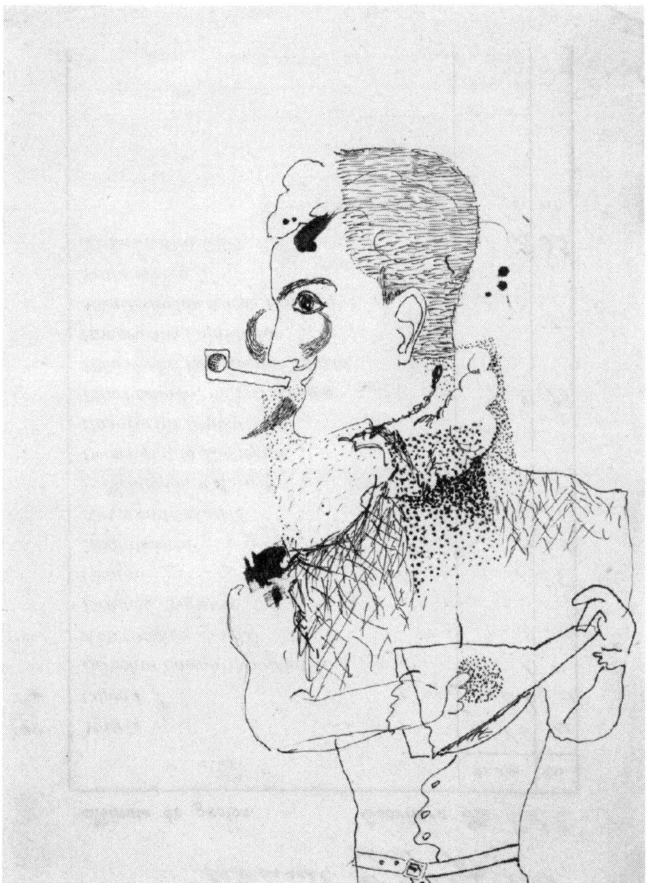

Salvador Dalí, pen and ink drawing of a *"putrefacto"* playing the mandolin, 1926-27

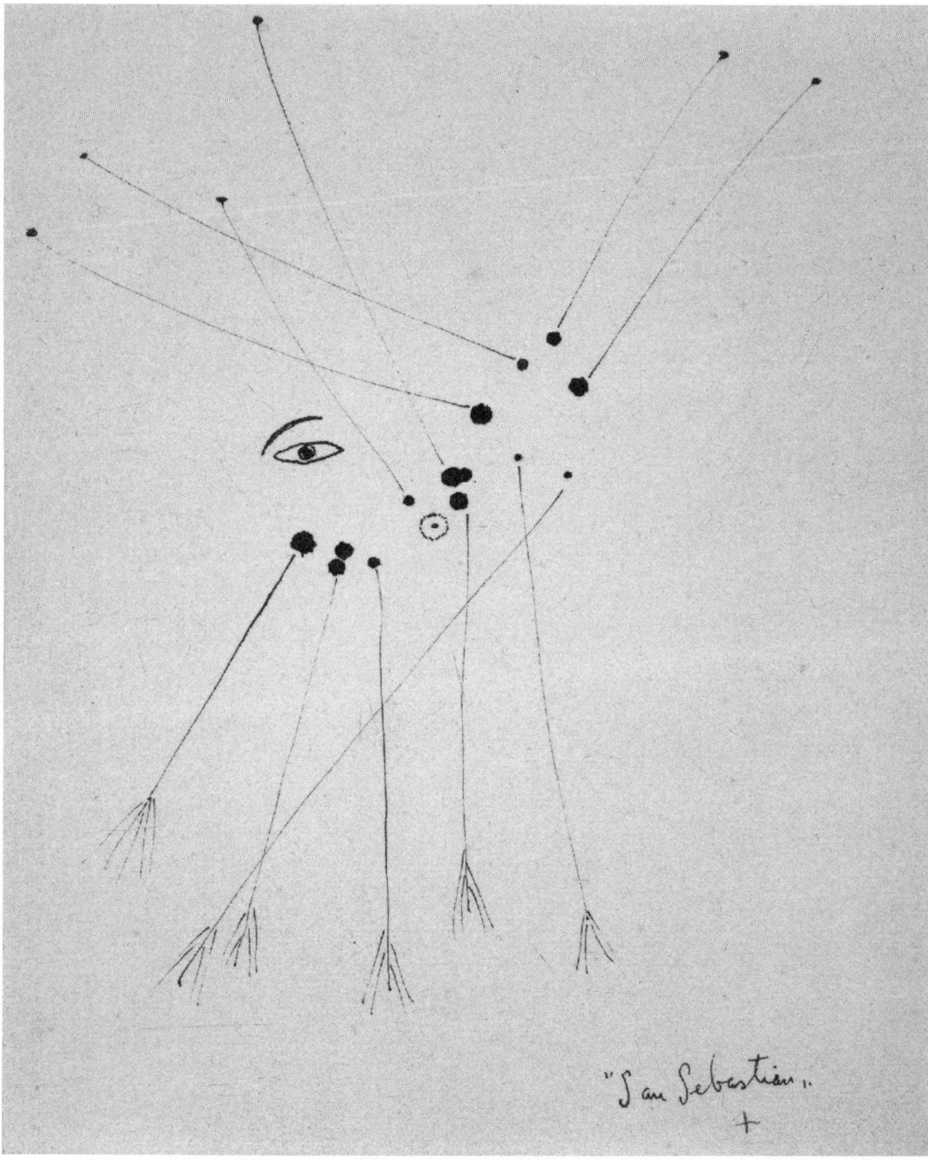

Federico García Lorca, *San Sebastián*, 1927. India ink on a piece of laid paper cut from a larger sheet. 155 x 125 mm. (Hernández no. 130)

Imagination, Inspiration, Evasion

Federico García Lorca

In an intimate gathering at the Residencia de Estudiantes, the architect Le Corbusier once said that what he had best liked about Spain was the expression *dar la estocada,* to make a clean kill, because it expressed the inner intention of going directly to the subject and the yearning to master it rapidly, without pausing over what is merely accessory and decorative.

I too believe in that doctrine, although, naturally, my sword is not a clean, agile one. The bull—the theme—lies before us, and we must kill it. At least that is my intention.

Imagination, inspiration, and evasion: the three degrees, the three steps traversed by any true work of art, by any poet conscious of the treasure God has given him, and, for that matter, by the whole of literary history.

Because I know how difficult this subject is, I am not trying to define, merely to emphasize. I don't want to delineate, I want to suggest. The mission of the poet is just that—to give life [*animar*], in the exact sense of the word: to give soul.... But don't ask me about truth or falsehood, because "poetic truth" is an expression which changes with the person to whom it is applied. Light in Dante can be ugliness in Mallarmé.

Furthermore, as everyone knows by now, one must *love* poetry. Poetry is like faith—it isn't meant to be understood but to be received in a state of grace. No one should say "this is clear," because poetry is obscure. And no one should say "this is obscure," because poetry is clear. What we must do is search out poetry energetically and virtuously so that it will surrender to us. We need to have forgotten poetry completely before it can fall naked into our arms. A state of poetic alert, and the people. What poetry cannot bear is indifference. Indifference is the devil's armchair. But it is indifference we hear babbling in the streets, dressed grotesquely in self-satisfaction and culture....

For me, imagination is synonymous with aptitude for discovery. To imagine, to discover, to carry our bit of light to the living penumbra where all the infinite possibilities, forms and numbers exist. I do not believe in creation but in discovery, and I don't believe in the seated artist but in the one who is walking the road. The imagination is a spiritual apparatus, a luminous explorer of the world it discovers. The imagination fixes and gives clear life to fragments of the invisible reality where man is stirring....

The imagination merely discovers things already created, it does not invent, and whenever it does so it is defeated by the beauty of reality. The imagination has its technique, with its own proper order and limits. It stalks its images using tried and true techniques of the hunt.... The mechanics of poetic imagination are always the same: a concentration, a leap, a flight, the hunt for imagery, a return with the treasure, and a classification and selection of what has been brought back. The poet dominates his imagination and sends it whatever he wants to. When he is not happy with its services he punishes it and sends it out again, just as the hunter punishes the dog that is too slow in bringing him the bird. Sometimes the hunt is splendid, but the most beautiful birds and the brightest lights almost always get away. For images are captured in reality.

The daughter of the imagination—the logical and legitimate daughter—is the metaphor, which is sometimes born from a sudden stroke of intuition and sometimes brought to light by the slow anguish of forethought.

But the imagination is limited by reality: one cannot imagine what does not exist. It needs objects, landscapes, numbers, planets, and it requires the purest sort of logic to relate those things to one another. One cannot leap into the abyss or do away altogether with the terms of reality. Imagination has horizons, it wants to delineate and make concrete all that lies within its reach.... The imagination hovers over reason the way fragrance hovers over a flower, without detaching itself from the petals, wafted on the breeze but tied, always, to the ineffable center of its origin....

The poetic imagination travels and transforms things, giving them their purest meaning, and it defines relationships no one had suspected. But it always, always, always works upon facts of a clear, specific reality.... It was imagination which discovered the four cardinal directions and which has discovered the intermediate causes of things, but imagination has never been able to rest its hands in the burning embers, without logic or sense, where one finds free, unrestrained inspiration. The imagination is the first stage, the foundation of all poetry, the cool, green, moonlit field where inspiration, liberated and alien to man, is about to spring into flight like an aeroplane, all insect wings and planetary nickel....

The poet uses imagination to build a tower against the elements and against mystery. It is unassailable. It orders and is listened to.... It is difficult for a so-called "pure" imaginative poet to produce intense emotion with his poetry. He *can*, of course, produce poetic emotions, and he can produce with the technique of verse that typical musical emotion of the Romantic, which falls short, almost always, of the deep spiritual meaning of the pure poet. (Heine was an example of a purely emotive poet, muted by the ironic tone with which he tried to justify his images.) But the imaginative poet cannot produce virginal, unrestrained, poetic emotion, free of walls—free-standing poetry with its own newly created laws. Imagination is poor, and the poetic imagination more so.

Visible reality, the facts of the world and of the human body are much more full of subtle nuances, and are much more poetic than what imagination discovers.

One notices this often in the struggle between scientific reality and imaginative myth, in which—thank God—science wins. For science is a thousand times more lyrical than any theogony.

The human imagination invented giants in order to explain the construction of great grottos or enchanted cities. Later, reality taught us that those great caves are made by the drop of water. The pure, patient, eternal drop of water. In this case, as in many others, reality wins. And the instinct of a drop of water is more beautiful than the hand of a giant. In poetry, real truth trumps imagination; that is, imagination discovers its own poverty. Imagination was about to attribute to giants what seemed the work of giants. But scientific reality, which is poetical in extreme and lies outside the ambit of logic, restored their truth to the perennial, pure drops of water. And it is, after all, much more beautiful that a cave be a mysterious caprice of water—chained and ordered by eternal laws—than the whim of giants who have no other meaning than that of an explanation.

The poet strolls through his imagination, limited by it. He knows that his imagination can be trained; that it can be enriched through a sort of imaginative gymnastics; that he can lengthen his radio waves and antennae of light. But the poet is sadly frustrated in his inner landscape.

He hears the flowing of great rivers. His forehead feels the cool of the reeds which tremble in the midst of "nowhere." He wants to hear the dialogue of the insects beneath the incredible boughs. He wants to penetrate the current of the sap in the dark silence of great tree trunks. He wants to understand the Morse alphabet spoken by the heart of the sleeping girl.

He wants. We all *want*. But that is precisely his sin: to *want*. One shouldn't *want*, one should *love*. When we love, we do not want. And so he fails. Because when he tries to express the poetic truth of any of these motifs, he will have to make use of human sentiment and of sensations he has seen and heard. He will use plastic analogies that will never be sufficiently expressive. For the imagination cannot reach those depths.

As long as he does not try to free himself from the world, the poet can live happily in his golden poverty. All the rhetorical systems, all the poetic schools in the world, from the Japanese on, have a lovely wardrobe of suns, moons, lilies, mirrors, and melancholy clouds for the use of all intelligences at all latitudes.

But the poet who wants to break free from the imagination, and not merely live on the images produced by real objects, stops dreaming and starts to desire. When the limits of his imagination become unbearable and he wants to free himself from his enemy—the World—he passes from desire to love. He goes from imagination, which is a fact of the soul, to inspiration, which is a state of the soul. He goes from analysis to faith.... And the poet, previously an explorer, is now a humble man who bears on his shoulders the irresistible beauty of all things. Here things exist "just because," with no explainable cause or effect. Here there are no limits, no bounds, only an admirable freedom.... Inspiration is a state of faith in the midst of the greatest possible humility. One needs to believe wholly in poetry, be in a state of spiritual and material grace, and reject the temptation to be understood. One must look through the eyes of a child and ask for the moon. One must ask for the moon and believe that they can put it in one's hands.

Often, inspiration directly attacks the intelligence and the natural order of things. Imagination assaults the theme furiously from all sides but inspiration receives it suddenly and wraps it in subtle, pulsing light, like those huge carnivorous flowers that envelop the trembling bee and dissolve it in the acrid juice exuded by their merciless petals.

Imagination is intelligent, orderly, full of equilibrium, but inspiration is sometimes incongruent—it does not recognize man, and often it places a livid worm in the clear eyes of our muse. Just because it *wants* to, without offering an explanation. Imagination creates a poetic atmosphere, and inspiration invents the "poetic fact"....

The poem that has evaded imaginative reality is no longer subject to the criteria of ugly or beautiful (as they are now understood) and it enters an amazing poetic reality which is sometimes full of tenderness and sometimes full of penetrating cruelty....

[Here the lecturer minutely analyzes the mechanism of inspiration, giving examples of some of the concepts he has expressed previously.... He goes on to analyze the "poetic fact".... He makes a rapid excursion through the miracles described by Jacobus de Voragine in *The Golden Legend,* and describes the legend of St. Bridget, beneath whose virginal fingers the wood of the altar filled with living echoes, flowering branches, and the nests of birds. The miracle is a form of pure emotion, it is inexplicable beauty. For additional examples he draws on his own *Gypsy Ballads*.... a book in which there are infinite, inexplicable, pure poetic facts, little noticed because they are in the line of imaginative poems.

Green I want you green,
Green wind, green boughs...

which has a strong popular flavor.

A thousand crystal tambourines
were wounding the dawn…

from "Death of Love" and other examples, which are not so inexplicable in their inner coherence as he himself imagines.]

Just as poetical imagination has a human logic, poetic inspiration has a poetic one. Acquired technique and aesthetic postulates are no longer of any use. And just as imagination is a discovery, inspiration is a gift, an ineffable gift…. It was Juan Larrea who said "This, which comes to me because of my innocence."

[The latest generation of poets has tried to reduce poetry to the creation of the "poetic fact" and to follow its norms, without listening to the voice of logical reasoning or the equilibrium of the imagination. These poets have tried to free poetry not only from anecdote but also from the riddle of the image, removing it from the plane of reality… in other words, take poetry to a higher level of purity and simplicity. This is a different reality, and they have tried to leap into a world of virgin emotions, suffuse their poems with a planetary feeling… and avoid any established aesthetics. Evasion of reality through dream, through the subconscious, through the path of some unheard-of "fact" given to the poet by inspiration…. Surrealism uses the dream, the intensely real world of dreams, and there one finds truly authentic poetic norms, but this evasion by means of dream or the subconscious is, although very pure, not very clear.]

We Spaniards want profiles and visible mystery. Form and sensuality.

In the north Surrealism can take hold—for example, modern German art— but Spain defends us from the strong liquor of dream.

Góngora is the perfect imaginative, verbal equilibrium and vivid line. He has no mystery and he is a stranger to insomnia. By contrast, San Juan de la Cruz is flight and yearning, yearning for perspective and unbounded love. Góngora is the academic, the terrible professor of language and poetry. San Juan de la Cruz will always be the disciple of the elements, the man who brushes the mountaintops with the soles of his feet.

The exaltation of Góngora which all of Spanish poetic youth has felt has coincided with the maturity of Cubism, a painting based on pure ratiocination, austere in color and arabesque, which culminated in Juan Gris, most Castilian of painters.

But in general, painters and poets, after the pure breeze of Cubism, turn their eyes to pure instinct, to uncontrolled virginal creation, to the cool source of direct emotion, resting on the irrepressible strength of their own newly discovered souls.

[He mentions the new values of Spanish poetry: Larrea and Diego ... who construct their poems from chains of poetic facts, which grow cleaner and cleaner and acquire a more crystalline flight.] Rafael Alberti has taken his poetry to a difficult, beautiful summit, where it breathes in eternal air. Opposite him, on the other bank, the prodigious magician Jorge Guillén gives his word a phosphorescent, mysterious, Machiavellian air, and Pedro Salinas, modest and enlightened, abandons his poems in an empty living room, where his cautious footsteps—those of a master—glisten in the dust. This school is a renaissance, a return to nature in reaction to the academicisms of the mature epoch of Cubism, which has been the most formidable of lessons in artistic discipline....

Plastic expression becomes poetic in order to take in vital juices and cleanse itself from the decorative ailments of the last of Cubism.

This is what I think—at present—of the poetry I am writing. When I say "at present" I mean today. Tomorrow, I don't know what I will think. Because I am a true poet, and will remain so until my death, I will never stop flagellating myself with the disciplines, and never give up hope that some day my body will run with green or yellow blood. Anything is better than to remain seated in the window looking out on the same landscape. The light of any poet is contradiction. I haven't tried to force my position on anyone—that would be unworthy of poetry. Poetry doesn't need skilled practitioners, she needs lovers, and she lays down brambles and shards of glass for the hands that search for her with love.

= Sketch de la nueva pintura =

el pintor

claridad

Monet decía: "Yo pinto como los pájaros cantan". Este era el [illegible] de las postrimerías pictóricas del siglo diecinueve. La luz y sus sorpresas [illegible] los cuadros agotando la belleza de la forma. Ya no existía la masa ni el puro [illegible] neto de los contornos. La magia de la luz caía sobre todos los objetos [illegible]. Reino del impresionismo. Mas que impresionismo se debería llamar sensacionismo o momentismo. Se exalta la belleza del instante por encima de todo. El [illegible] sirve de canon, contra el plinto de mármol. Es la época en que se miran los cuadros haciendo un embudo con la mano delante del ojo y en que una cara [illegible] nos una mancha que toma apariencia de cara. La naturaleza es tan pequeña [illegible] en su gama de colores. Los pintores se recrean en sus lejanías y en sus humos, [illegible] que el menor control inteligente intervenga en esta borrachera de copiar los espectáculos naturales. La pintura agonizaba. Comienza la reacción y con la reacción se inicia su salvamento y su cambio total de sentido.

Los últimos impresionistas se detuvieron en el borde mortal y empezaron a [illegible] a los grandes maestros clásicos. Había que volver por el volumen, por la forma, fundamento esencial de un cuadro. Se había perdido el esqueleto y la pintura era una gelatina [illegible] que irritaba nuestra emoción y nuestro sentido de virgen la belleza. Fue Cézanne el que dijo a un modelo esta frase histórica poco después: "Es[illegible] usted quieto señor: yo lo pinto a usted lo mismo que pinto una manzana". De Cézanne arranca el afán constructivo que ha de renovar la pintura hasta que llega el andamiaje a un extremo agudo por Ozenfant y Jeanneret con el [illegible] titulado Purismo y a un extremo científico por los Constructivistas que afirman "que entre la matemática y el arte, que entre un objeto de arte y una invención técnica no se pueden determinar los límites", se abre en la pintura una reacción anímica, un modo espiritualista en el crear: las imágenes ya no son dadas por la inteligencia, sino por el inconsciente, por la pura inspiración directa.

Manuscript page of "Sketch of the New Painting"

Sketch of the New Painting

Federico García Lorca

The painter Claude Monet used to say: "I paint the way birds sing." This was the motto of the final days of nineteenth century painting. Light and its surprises had invaded pictures, exhausting the beauty of form. Mass no longer existed, or a pure, clean sense of contour. The magic of light fell on objects, destroying them. The reign of Impressionism. Rather than Impressionism, it ought to have been called Sensationalism or Momentism. The beauty of the instant matters more than anything else. The fleeting river serves as canon, and not the marble plinth. This is a time when people look at paintings by making their hand into a funnel and holding it in front of the eye; a time when a face is no more than a blot with the appearance of a face. Nature is clumsily imitated over its entire gamut of colors. Painters rejoice in their distances and their smoke, until not the slightest bit of intelligent control intervenes in this drunken orgy of copying natural spectacles. Painting is in its death throes. A reaction sets in, bringing about the salvation of painting and a total change of direction. The last of the Impressionists pull up on the fatal brink, and begin to copy the great masters and classics. It was time to return to volume and form, the essential foundation of painting. The skeleton had been lost, and painting had become a gelatin that irritated our emotion and our virgin sense of beauty. It was Cézanne who, a little later, uttered these historic words to a model: "Please sit still. I am painting you the way I paint an apple."

From Cézanne came the constructive yearning that would renew painting. Its scaffolding reached acute extremes in Ozenfant and Jeanneret with the style titled Purism, and it reached scientific extremes in Constructivism, which affirms that "one cannot determine the boundary between mathematics and art, and between an object of art and a technical invention." All this brought about an animical reaction, a spiritualist mode where images are no longer produced by the imagination, rather by the unconscious—by pure, direct inspiration.

Classical painting had always portrayed nature or a conventional reality of nature. Eyes were enslaved to what they saw, and the soul of the painter was a sad creature chained to these eyes, without its own criteria or a freedom like that of the poet and the musician.

A Perseus was needed to slay the monster and break the sad chains of this ancient Andromeda.

In the year 1909, the first Cubist painting was shown in a salon. If I were to share with you all the anecdotes and gossip that surrounded it, I would need three days, and since this is a simple, badly drawn "sketch," there is no time for that. Suffice it to say that the framers refused to frame it and the apprentices to transport it. Who would have said that eight years later a Cubist painting would be sold for 300,000 francs?

When the first Cubist painting appeared, an abyss opened between the old and the new painting. For the first time, despite all of their living essences and eternal marvels, a whole multitude of museum painters become merely "historic." A struggle began between the old and the new. Since Picasso was painting like *this*, in an admirable manner from a realistic point of view (slide of old woman with the eye and Aragonese girl), in this quintessentially Spanish painting, picturesque and, thank god, now dead (he removes the slide), and since Braque had a magnificent talent, people began to say and with them, great artists from the other arts—that Picasso and the Cubists wanted to play a practical joke on people and drive mad people of good faith. And what good faith! They were carrying out the greatest, most purifying, most liberating work in the history of painting. They were saving painting, which was an art of representation, and turning it into an art in itself, a pure art, free of reality. In historical painting, color and volume had been at the service of the portrait, the religious picture. In modern painting color and volume begin—for the first time ever—to live their own feelings and to communicate and interact on the canvas, obeying the laws dictated by their essences.

Guillaume Apollinaire and Max Jacob began a similar movement in poetry, but it was painters like Pablo Picasso, the genial painter from Málaga, who really explored undiscovered paths.

It is *painting* which cries out loud, which affirms, and which moves the world, because it is painting which is seen by all eyes; painting which appeared on every front in Europe, perturbing people and arousing their emotions, like anything that is alive and carries warm blood in its bosom.

The year 1914. The Great War destroys "real" reality. One stares at it in disbelief. There is no reasoning which can resist war. The visible does not seem authentic. Ethical constructions come tumbling down. What we once believed, we no longer believe. All chains are broken, and the stray soul finds itself alone and bare, owner of its own perspective. No need to pay attention to eyes that deceive. We must free ourselves from this natural reality in order to search for true plastic reality. Not search for the effective qualities of things, but for their natural plastic equivalences. Not search for the real representation of an object, but find its pictorial expression, its geometrical or lyrical expression, and the appropriate quality of its material. The Great War is the mother of the new painting. Amid that pain, amid that reality, conquered by the incredible, painting ceases to be the slave of the senses and becomes autonomous. For five centuries, people had been painting in the same way. Now, all of a sudden, they turn toward a more logical north, one more in harmony with the meaning of creation.

It is another Spaniard, Juan Gris, who says in a famous lecture at the Sorbonne: "To paint a glass bottle exactly, with the quality it really has, is very easy, and the bottle maker does it much better. I am looking for the pictorial expression of the glass, and the pictorial material of the glass, but not for its visual reality." And to be sure, objects have certain outer appearances and resonances that are not pictorial, and which the painter ought to suppress because they are useless and harmful. For example, patches of reflected light—those disgusting blobs of white paint so many naturalist painters apply to objects are the greatest bit of plastic nonsense that ever existed, since the brilliance is a fleeting tremor, external to the object, and does not form part of its line or volume and is alien to its nature. Clearly these painters are wanting people to say "Jones has painted Smith, and got him exactly right. If I were by myself with that picture in a room, it would scare me to death," etc., things like that, alien to painting.

And so, fleeing from the destruction of the Impressionists, one gets to the Franciscan school of the Cubists. The Impressionists' infinite roses and greys and silvers, their greens, reds, yellows (across the spectrum in their violet deliquescences, their chiaroscuros and sfumatura), and their infinite roses and greys and silvers, give way to white, sienna, tobacco, and the mute, austere colors of the Cubist palette. The orgy of color is muted and—even more important—there is no longer a theme, which used to be the very foundation of historical painting. "This picture represents such and such," one used to say. But we are now in a world apart. "This is a picture that represents nothing more than a picture," one says nowadays. Just as a sonnet, from the poetical point of view, represents nothing more than a sonnet and a chair nothing more than a chair. But what does it say? What does it express? Well, that's something else. A grey sets up a background where various forms and volumes in harmony (in beauty), felt by the painter, are at play and interact according to their natures, giving origin to a world which moves us or makes us think.

The painter has departed from reality in order to get to this sort of creation. The same as a poet creates the image he defines, the painter creates the plastic image that fixes and guides the emotion. He has enough with one or two objects. He uses them as a starting point and recreates them, or better said, discovers their intimacy, their pictorial marrow, unseen by the copyist.

The Cubists have been austere in their creations. They have composed the majority of their still lifes with a guitar or violin, an apple, a plaster hand and a sea dog's pipe.

But they have given these objects thousands of expressions, working with the most sensual—divine, granular materials that make one want to eat them, or pass one's hand over them; oil paintings combined with fine sand, with a sumptuous life, painted by George Braque, very close in quality to the splendid texture of the sports clothes manufactured by the English, or schematic, cold, unfleshed expressions, which approach the perfect emotion of a claire de lune, as in the guitars, interlaced with that delicate sense of nocturnal fish, that come from the hand of our Juan Gris. Pure matter, pure form and pure color. How far, how free from the pictorial concept that the portrait painter used to have!

Painting is now free, elevated to the spiritual rank of the arts that are arts in themselves, those which, free of all exterior agents, find their own deep, complete resonance.

Picasso and Georges Braque are the leaders of the war generation, and it is they who have brought to life the tree trunk of Cubism, whose final branch, pure and definitive, already in heaven, has been Juan Gris. And from that trunk come all the constructive and truly pictorial modes of modern painting.

Together with Cubism which—we will always say—went beyond painting and was a totally new, unsuspected creation within the plastic arts, there arise various other schools that have used the language of color to bring about—careful!—not *plastic* creation of the sort one tries for at this blessed moment, but *literature.* Often, they have created *bad* literature. Such is Italian Futurism. Futurism exalts movement, it wants to make its paintings tremble on the crest, the vertex of an unfettered dynamism. It hates the statue and adores the runaway horse. It brings together outer sensations with inner ones, and, in sum, it is nothing more than the exaltation of the *gesture.* Nothing more genuinely Italian! Between a Futurist and a speaker at a political rally there isn't a great deal of difference. Marinetti, the founder, is just that—a delightful orator who has been brave enough to use strong language on solemn occasions. Balla, Carrà, Soffici—Futurist painters—had more talent than Marinetti, but Futurism has no raison d'etre, given the existence of cinema. Cinema has brought to life for our eyes the spectacle that the Futurists were unable to produce with their canvases. A Fox newsreel of the sort we see every week in the movies is superior to all the creations of these admirable Italians who did so much to awaken their country and who wanted to burn the museums and smash Michelangelo's *David* in order to save Italy from the horrors of tourism, that makes her weep and tremble under the eyes of people who have no more idea of art than "this painting is worth four million," "this pulpit would go for 400,000 pounds."

In the middle of the war, Dadaism arose—and I think Dadaism too is literary painting. Works were created for a single minute. The Dadaists faced down all of art, with the greatest joy, and they neither affirmed nor denied. It was a great, necessary purge, and those who pulled it off are marvelously ingenious people. But one must admit that Dadaism, for all the scandal it provoked, was nothing more than the flower of a day, though it produced good results considering all that it destroyed.

Futurism and Dadaism have been conflicting, scandalous movements, mixed up with the political ideas and movements of cities. But while the Dadaists were dispersing in order to go back to their old disciplines or try new ones, Marinetti has taken Futurism to an official consecration in which the other great Futurist, Mussolini, gave him an embrace under the sixty-meter flag given him by the people of Milan.

After the war, painters either followed the Cubist discipline, taking it to extremes of science, like the Purists or Constructivists, or they embarked on a social painting which castigated vices, like the German Verists, the unbearable Verists. Others made painting an expressive exaltation of things, pushing objects to their final limits and contours and capturing their spirit, as did the Expressionists who enlivened the city of Berlin. A multitude of "isms" took over. Some are literary, and who can doubt that they had useful artistic beauty? Others are purely pictorial and plastic—those which follow and cluster around Cubism. Discipline that went on in the studio, without excessive public commotion, works of meditated maturity exhibited to the public.

And thus the truly regenerative movement has been Cubism in its three epochs. Discipline, love, law. Death of perspective and abstract exaltation of volume. This is its profile.

And then we get to 1926. The Cubist lesson has already been

fully utilized. But a sad cerebralism, a tired intellectualism has invaded painting. Severini and Gris already know a picture by memory before they even paint it. Where are we heading? Toward instinct, chance, pure inspiration, the fragrance of the direct.

The Surrealists come onto the scene, and surrender themselves to the inner pulse of the soul. And painting emancipated from the disciplined abstractions of Cubism, master of an immense, centuries-old technique, enters a mystical, uncontrolled period of supreme beauty. The Surrealists set about expressing the inexpressible. In a new domain, which seems immortal, the sea fits inside an orange and a tiny insect can awaken wonder in the planetary rhythm, where a horse at rest carries a troubling footprint in its staring eyes.

After reaching an acute objectivism in 1920, today painting has come, wise and old, to a lyrical field where—following a necessary biological process—it will shed its skin, and become a child, daughter of stylized cave painting, first cousin of the exquisite art of savage peoples.

It is our glory, as Spaniards, to have produced the three great revolutionary painters in the world today. The father of all living painters is the Andalusian Pablo Picasso. The man who has created the theology and academy of Cubism is Juan Gris, from Madrid. And the divine poet and painter Joan Miró is a son of Cataluña. In each of them, their nationality is obvious. Picasso is the genial Andalusian who invents miraculously, and has the most surprising intuition, and Juan Gris is Castile—reason and ardent faith. He converted to Cubism and never did anything else until his death, which occurred last year. While Picasso was painting Cubist canvases and was doing paintings in the manner of Goya, or painting a Fragonard or a Mantegna with his prodigious technique, Juan Gris was a grey man who studied his paintings and never altered his dogma. Joan Miró is more European and his art is now absolutely unclassifiable: it partakes of astronomy and eludes any one nationality. But there is no doubt that Spain goes on producing its geniuses. The Spanish genius, with eternal life, which revives and awakens all activities bathing them in its own peculiar, unheard of light.

I have no time in this note to go on at length, as I would like to. The theme is a broad one, and this is only an exhibition, a brief *sketch* of the new painting. The theme is infinitely suggestive but we have to set limits. Nor do I want to tire the audience with quotations or the names of a multitude of new artists. No one has surpassed these three figures, the ones I spoke of a moment ago. Now we are going to show a few slides. Not too many, so as not to tire you out.

Impressionism

1. Renoir

2. Cézanne

Cubism

3. Picasso

4. Picasso

5. Gleizes

6. Juan Gris

7. Léger (decorative)

8. Ozenfant, aseptic, where it is already a scientific theorem

9. Proun: extends painting to architecture

Futurism

10. Severini 1913

11. Balla

Orphic Cubism

12. Kandinsky

Dada

13. Picabia

One begins to note the influence of poetry in the painting of Giorgio [di] Chirico. He is a strange painter who owes much to the Cubists and creates something he calls metaphysical painting which tries to resolve the following problem: representing the immaterial by the material. From my point of view, he achieves it.

I believe that Chirico produces a new emotion of uncanniness, of solitude, of terror with his paintings. Jean Cocteau, the delightful French poet has said: "Chirico or the scene of the crime, Chirico at the hour of the train." Sure enough, his paintings have that anguish. Paintings with a strange, mortal air.

14.

15.

And let's look at a few examples of Surrealism. Here is the young painter Dalí, lightly influenced by Chirico:

16.

17.

18.

Light

In these last few paintings by Miró we have been in the presence of the purest art that has ever been invented since man took up the brush. This statement could be demonstrated both historically and aesthetically.

This nocturnal landscape where insects speak with one another, and this other panorama, or whatever (I don't care what it is, and don't need to know) are on the verge of not having existed. They come from dream, from living flesh, from the center of the soul, with love and breezes and distant murmurs. Looking at these paintings I experience the same mysterious, terrible emotion I feel at the bullfight at the moment they drive a dagger into the neck of the lovely animal—the moment when we peer over the edge into death, which sinks its steel beak into the tender, intangible trembling of the grey matter.

I have no doubt that "modern painting" is a tangible phenomenon which extends to every country in the world. As with any great movement, we coincide—without reaching agreement—all over the world. And the proof of the overwhelming force which the movement has is the attitude of the old painting, whose expositions no longer interest anyone, and the fear and sordidness of the old sleight-of-hand painters who do not want to see, or hear, in their failures, and who shut themselves away to copy the marvelous and uncopiable reality that they destroy in their canvases. The old painting is now beating a dramatic sort of retreat. And there are cases, like that of great painter from Granada, the noblest in material and the one with the best taste, in my judgement, who, finding himself in the midst of the earthquake, rather than beginning a new plastic discipline (here he is mistaken) and hating with all his soul his old manner, ceased nobly to paint, in hopes that peoples' sensibilities would change. This reveals one of the most select spirits imaginable, but it also reveals the failure of nineteenth century painting, and with it, all historical painting. One has painted in every way possible, admirably, prodigiously. The new painting, still in its swaddling clothes, is beginning a new path, and one must encourage it.

It is impossible for art to mineralize, and I feel true pity for the artists who do not struggle or subject themselves to discipline and dream of impossible things that they want to realize. I feel infinite pity for all the old painters who, with neither effort nor happiness nor pain, earn their sad daily bread copying and recopying their models.

I would burn their canvases, and toss them out onto the street, to struggle with the fire of man and the impassioned love of God.

Art must advance just as science advances, day after day, toward making the incredible believable, and toward the things that seem absurd but which change later into a pure hard edge of truth.

Before finishing I would like to say that our position is an honorable one. We all have faith in what we have said, and neither the laughter of the ignorant, nor being labeled crazy or other things, matter to us at all. Not at all.

The faith and joy of a new, future epoch are fixed in our consciousness. Ladies and gentlemen, the *sketch* of modern painting has ended.

26 October 1928

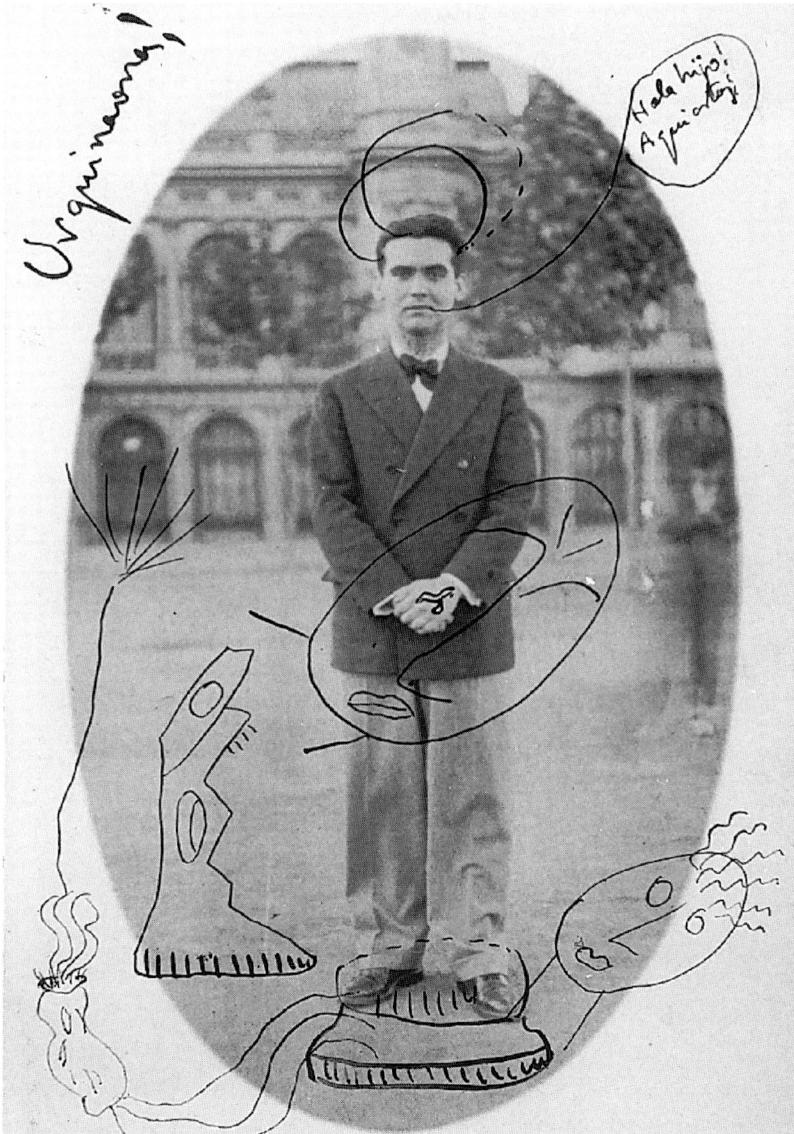

Federico García Lorca, *Urquinaona!* Photo with drawing, 131 x 90 mm (Hernández no. 98). Collection Casa Museo Federico García Lorca, Fuentevaqueros, Granada. From Urquinaona Plaza, Barcelona, Lorca announces his presence to Dalí: "Hola hijo! / Aquí estoy" (Hello, son! Here I am!). The posture is reminiscent of that of St. Sebastian (note the halo), and the figure to Lorca's right would remind Dalí of one of his own "apparatuses."

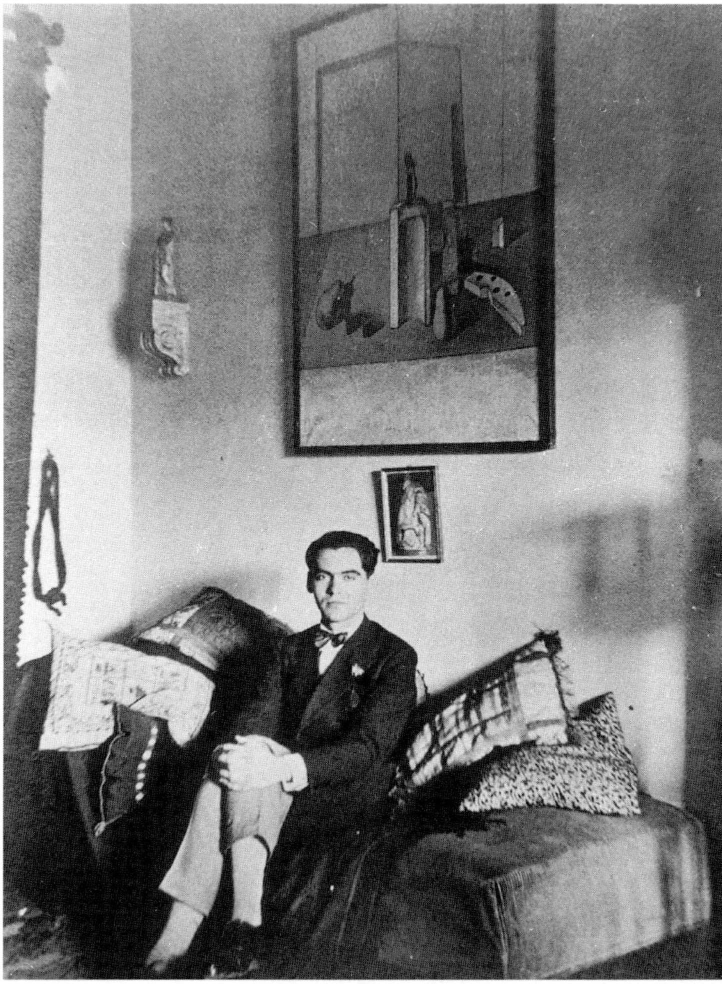

Federico García Lorca in his room at the Residencia de Estudiantes, Madrid, c. 1927. On the wall is Dalí's *Purist Still Life*, 1924 (D 184) which the painter had given him after exhibiting it at the first exhibition of the Sociedad de Artistas Ibéricos in May and June, 1925. The painting is now in the Museo Nacional Reina Sofía Madrid. The Spanish poet Mario Hernández remarks of this photo: "One of the loveliest photographic portraits of Lorca. He has dated it in Granada, 1927, in the copy made for his English friend Campbell Hackforth-Jones. The friend had visited him in Granada during Christmas vacation, 1926, and it seems likely that the picture and dedication are from January, 1927, toward the end of his stay. To the left, on the Turkish bed on which the poet is sitting, is an exquisite embroidered pillow which must have been done by the poet's mother, a master of the art. The year that the pillow was embroidered, 1924, is visible. The Cubist still life by Dalí hanging on the wall must have been given [by Dalí] to Lorca in 1924 or 1925, together with a "Nude" that was shown in the same exhibition."

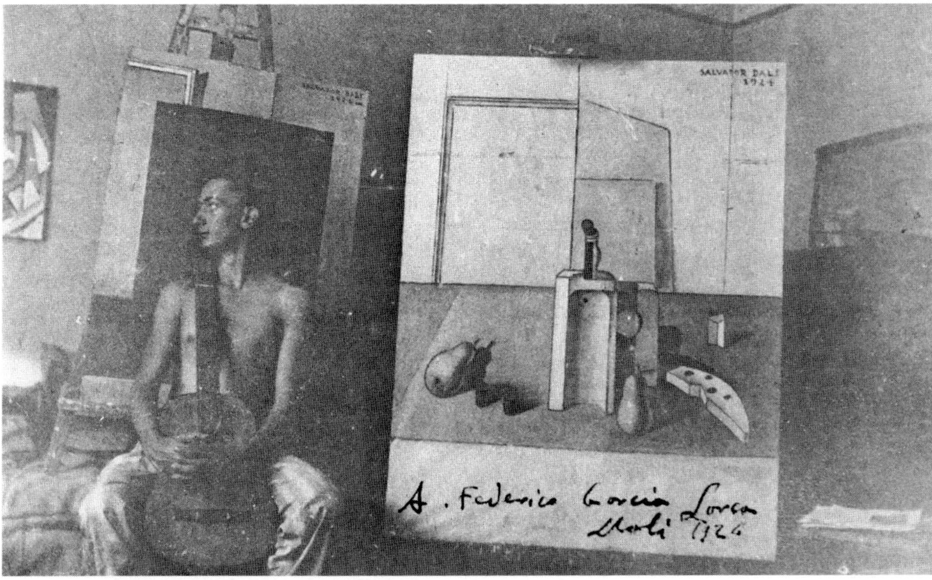

Salvador Dalí in his studio in Figueres, beside his painting *Purist Still Life*, 1924. The photo is dedicated "To Federico García Lorca, Dalí, 1924."

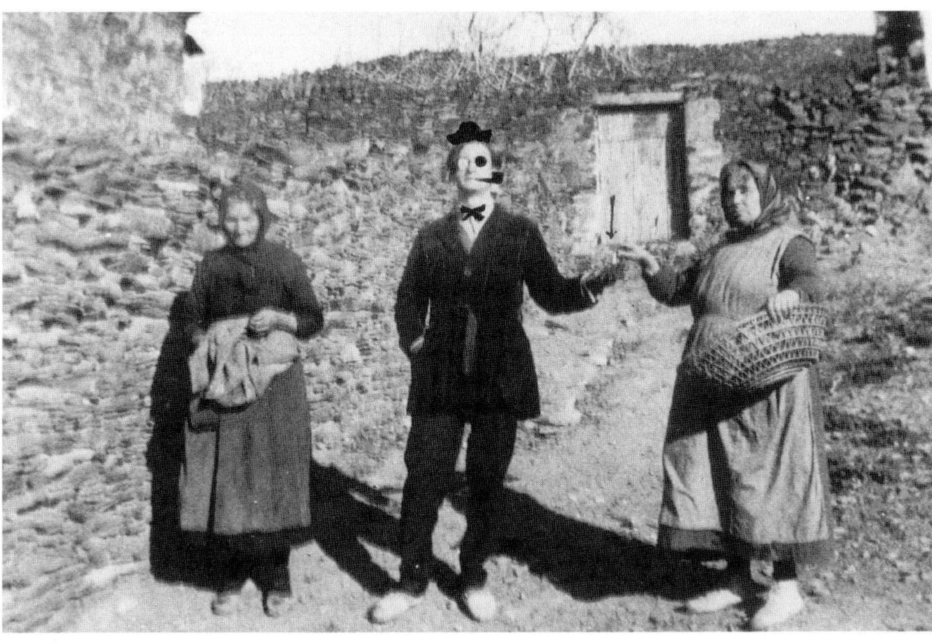

Dalí has titled the photo "Lidia gives me a fish," and dates it "Día de Reyes, Cadaqués". A caption (not visible here) reads "La Patum, yo, la Lidia (La Bien Plantada). To Federico García Lorca who is in on the secret. Dalí."

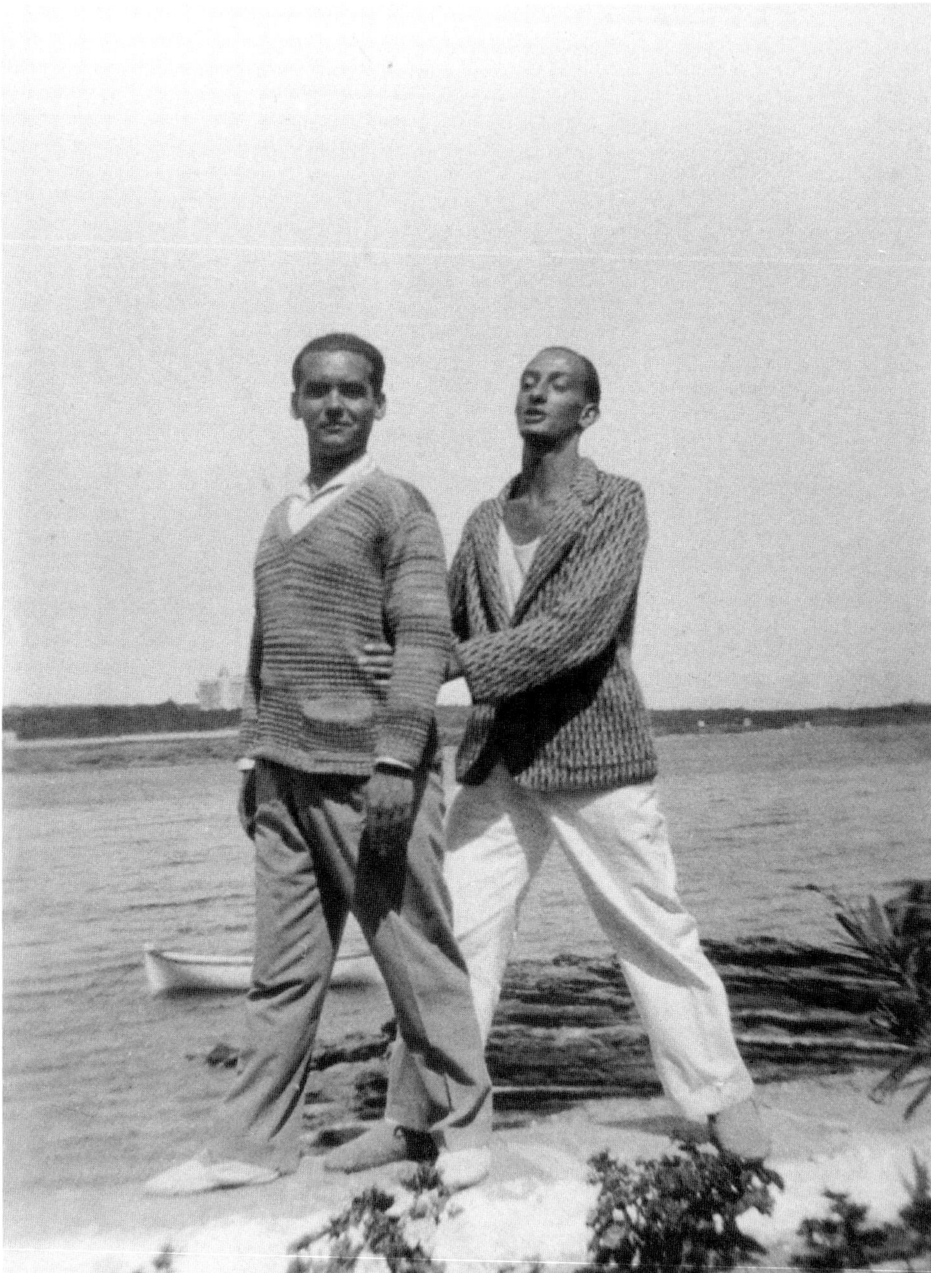

Federico García Lorca and **Salvador Dalí** on the beach in Cadaqués, summer 1927.

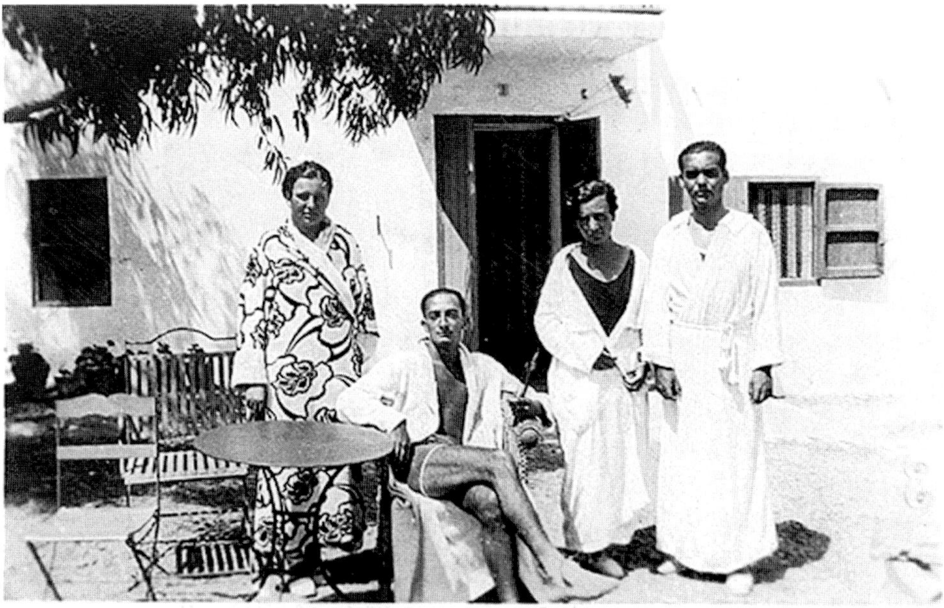

Cadaqués, summer 1927, on the terrace at the Dalí family's home in Cadaqués. Dalí is seated at the table. To his left are Anna Maria and Federico.

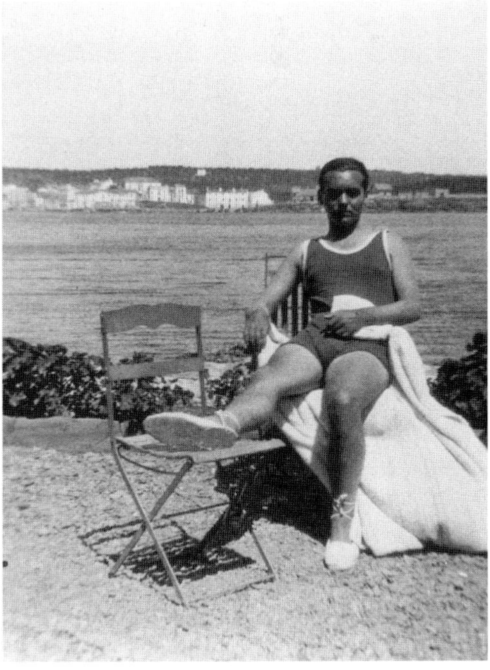

Federico García Lorca on the terrace at the Dalí family's home in Cadaqués.

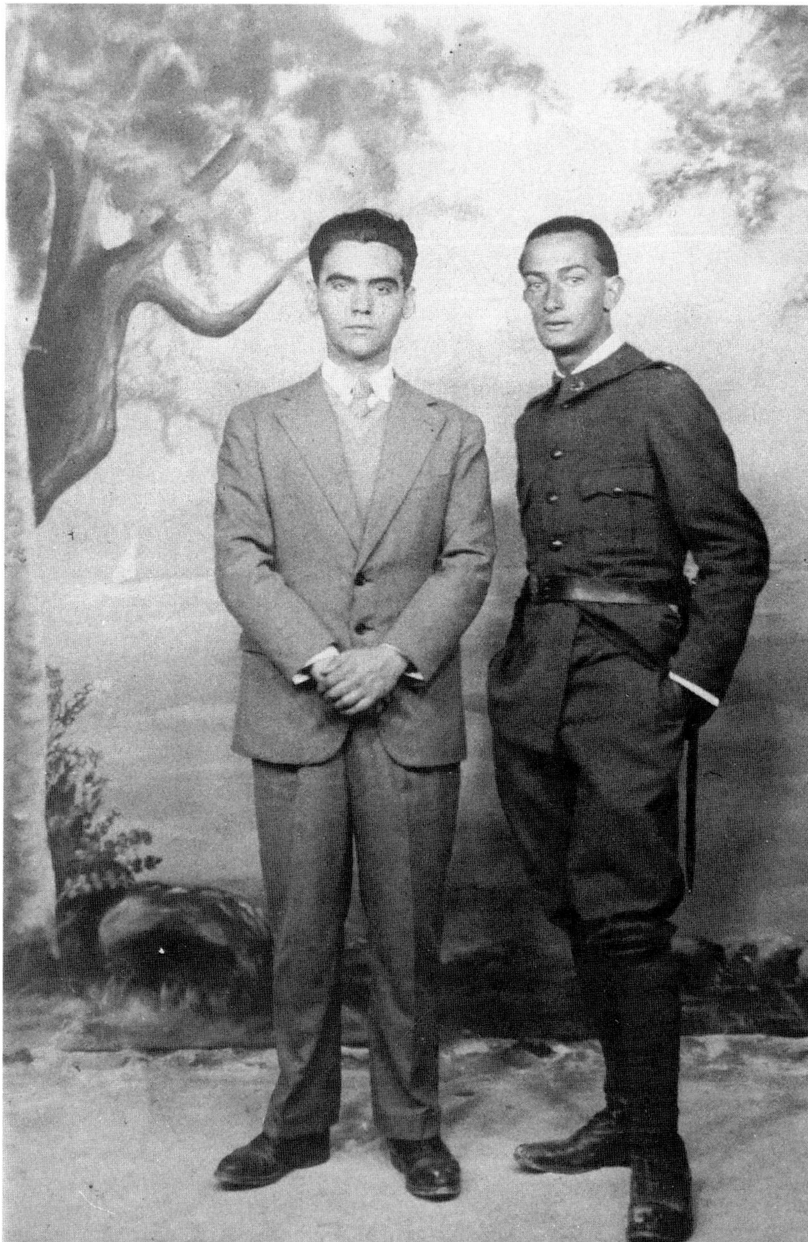

Federico García Lorca and **Salvador Dalí**, Figueres, 1927, with Dalí dressed in his military uniform. "You won't believe this, but for the past month I've been a soldier. I haven't mentioned it until now because it's a very long story, but anyway I love it, it's so strange."

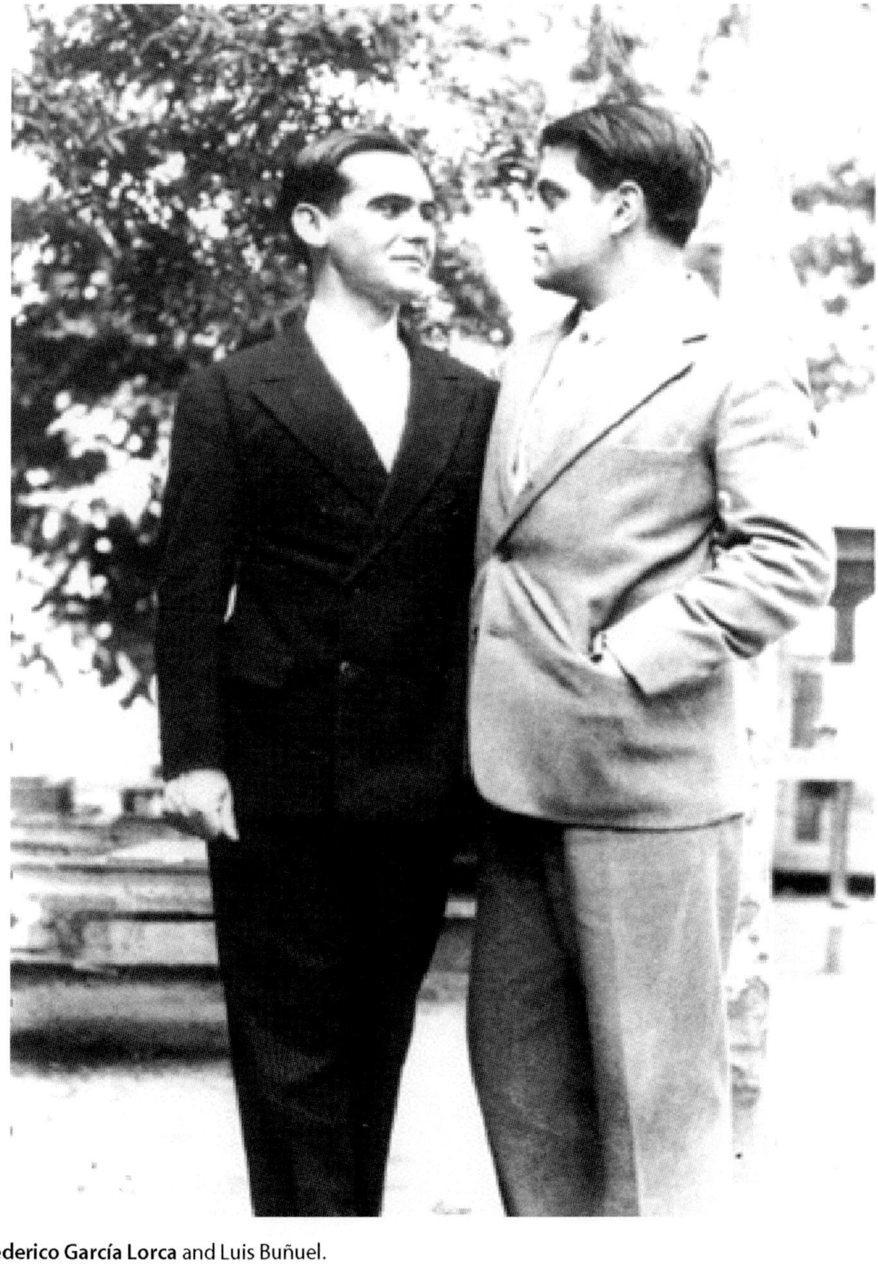

Federico García Lorca and Luis Buñuel.

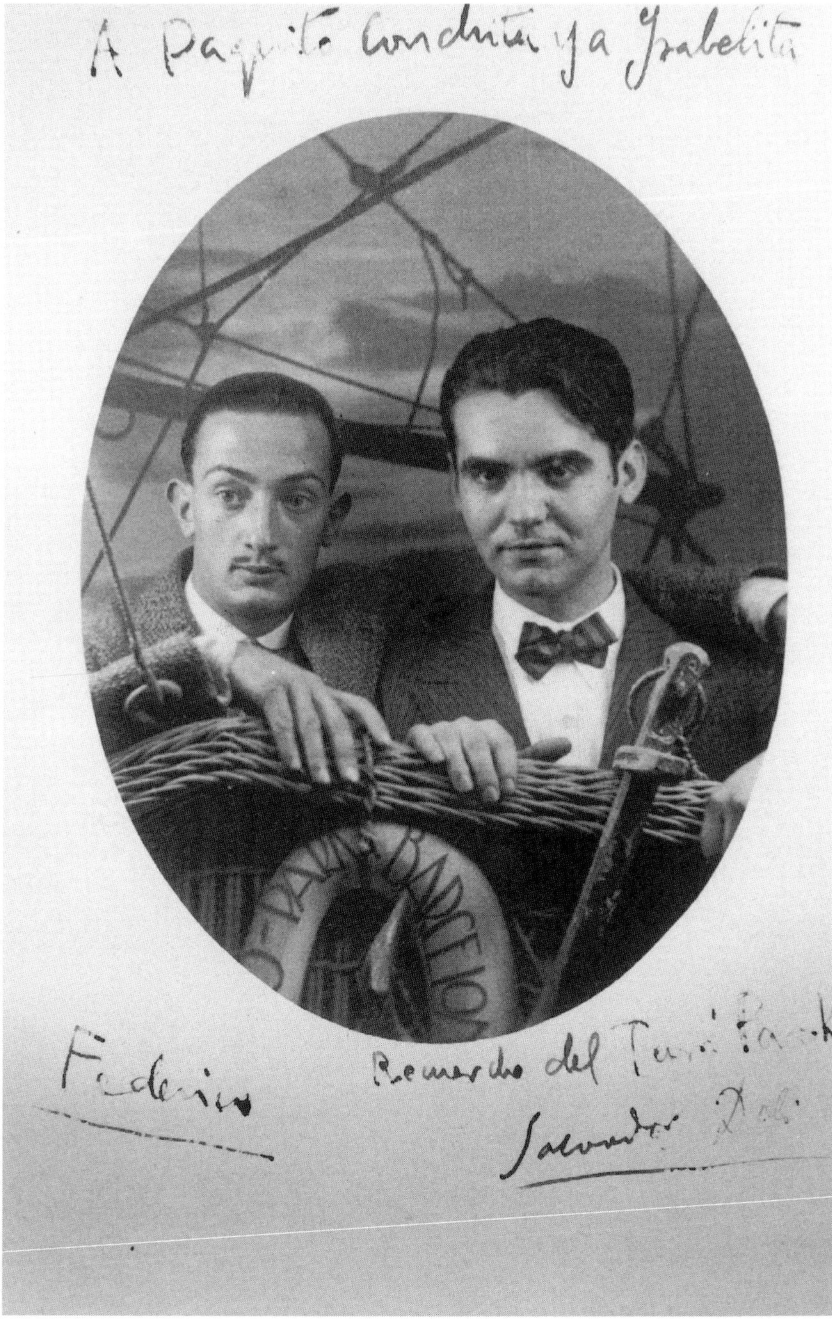

Dalí and Lorca at an amusement park, Holy Week, 1925. The photo is dedicated by Lorca to his brother Paquito (Francisco) and his two sisters, Concha and Isabel.

Notes

The brief notes which follow aim merely to clarify names and terms unfamiliar to the English reader. More detailed commentaries are available in the works of Ades, Anderson, Finkelstein, Gaillemin, Gibson, Santos Torroella, and other critics.

Prologue

Anti-Art. In a letter to Sebastià Gasch, Dalí writes: "'Artistic'—horrible word that only serves to indicate things totally lacking in art. Artistic performance, artistic photography, artistic advertisement, artistic furniture. Horror! Horror! What we all like, on the other hand, is the *purely industrial* object, dance-halls and the quintessential poetry of Buster Keaton's hat" (*Shameful Life* 192).

Head of Lorca superimposed on that of Dalí. See Santos Torroella 1984 and Hernández 1989. For an opposing view, Fanés 1998.

All men like St. Sebastian "when they criticize us": Gaillemen (58) points out that "La vision de l'artiste comme être douloureux et incompris, en proie aux flèches de la critique et à l'incompréhension du public, est un lieu commun romantique que l'on peut rapprocher de certains autoportraits en Christ souffrant [...] Sébastien incarne également l'attitude de l'artiste en face de la nature. C'est ainsi que l'on peut interpréter les Sébastien de Redon dans les années 1910-1912."

Attempt at sodomy: Dalí continues: "Deep down I said to myself that he was a very great poet and that I owed him a bit of the Divine Dalí's ar—! He ended up by using a girl, and she replaced me in the sacrifice. Not having succeeded in persuading me to put my ar— at his disposal, he swore to me that the sacrifice exacted from the girl was compensated by his own: it was the first time he'd had intercourse with a woman." Gibson, who accepts the truth of Dalí's account, and spoke to him about it in 1986, writes that the "girl" in question was Margarita Manso (*Shameful Life*, 178-79, 669)

Buñuel reaction to Lorca. Gibson (*Shameful Life* 217) quotes from a letter of September 1927 from Buñuel to Pepín Bello: "Federico sticks in my craw incredibly. I thought that the boyfriend [Dalí] was putrescent, but now I see that the other is even worse. It's his awful aestheticism that has distanced him from us. His extreme narcissism was already enough to make a pure friendship with him impossible. Anyway, it's his problem. The trouble is that his work may suffer as a result. // Dalí is deeply under his influence. He believes himself to be a genius, thanks to the love Federico professes for him. He's written to me saying: 'Federico is better than ever. He's *the* great man, his drawings have genius. I'm producing amazing work, etc.' And then, of course, his successes in Barcelona are so easily achieved. How I'd love to see him arrive here [in France] and renew himself far from the influence of the nefarious García! Because, and it's a fact, Dalí is a real male and very talented."

"fragment published in the Gaceta": "Degollación de los Inocentes" (Beheading of the Innocent), *La Gaceta Literaria* (Madrid), III, no. 50 (15 January 1929), 1. See Anderson, ed., *Poemas en prosa* 81-83 and the translation by Sawyer-Lauçanno, 39-41.

Letters

1.

Lorca is apologizing because he had taken over a month to write Anna María Dalí after his visit of 1925 to the Dalí family in Cadaqués. During that visit he had written to his family an enthusiastic letter (April 8, 1925) which casts light on the letter to Anna María and which deserves to be reproduced in full:

> Dear parents, brother and sisters: // I am in Cadaqués, a little town in Gerona, as I said, and one of the marvels of the Mediterranean. You can't imagine—accustomed as you are to the sea at Málaga—this "Costa Brava" sea full of inlets, harbors and ravines in which one sees huge olive trees and vineyards, orange-colored rocks, and green splotches of pine forest. It is marvelous! The trip to Barcelona is pretty because one goes through the dry, delirious land of Aragón—bare rock and old anguish of Spain—and traverses this stupendous, wealthy Cataluña, an admirable region which, from now on, has all my sympathy. Dalí's family has received me exquisitely. The father is a very learned man who knows an infinite number of my poems by

memory. They are taking delightfully good care of me and have done some really kind things for me. I'm only sorry that you can't see with me these seas and this land of the Ampurdá, full of Greek things and with an elegance and an antiquity that you would find as amazing as I do. // Today we made a trip to Cabo Creus and the coast of France with two fishermen named Filemón and Bancis. Dear Paquito, isn't this like an ecglogue of Hesiod? During the sea trip, which lasted the whole day, the fishermen told some intensely simple and poetic tales. Filemón is a young man of twenty years, melancholy and reserved. He narrated classical tales of witches and of love, while the lateen sail trembled against the sky blue, green and lapis lazuli of the Mediterranean. Bancis is a man of thirty Aprils, humoristic and shy, who spoke of human and divine affairs with surprising wit and joy. "Tomorrow they kill our Lord," he said, with a certain irony... He spoke of other priests and people of the village with a sort of exclusively Catalan humor. On our return, the sea was rough and I got home with a mask of ocean salt. Tomorrow, Good Thursday, they're taking me to Gerona to see the liturgy in the Cathedral and the Monday after Easter I will give a reading, probably in Barcelona, which the people at the Atheneum are greatly looking forward to. Before Barcelona I will have to read in the Library of the Mancomunidad de Figueras—just today a young author came to Cadaqués to invite me in the name of all of them. I'll do this, because these people have been so splendidly kind to me. Spain is dead, but Cataluña is alive, and because it is alive there is political and social and literary life. This is what I've been able to observe during my brief stay here. In Barcelona, I'll speak with that shameless fox Martínez Sierra. And I'll keep you posted. // *Bona nit* [good night], my dear ones. Remember me as I do you. Above all I remember Mamá because I know how she loves the ocean. Mamá, what a beautiful sea this is! I'll breathe it in deeply, both for you and for me. Goodbye. Write me—Salvador Dalí House, Cadaqués, Gerona—as soon as this letter arrives. Hugs and kisses. // FEDERICO

Divine Shepherdess: a religious print Lorca had given Dalí at the Residencia de Estudiantes whose style reminded Dalí of the *Douanier* Rousseau (*See* letter 3) (RST, *SD escribe,* 118)

Auntie: Catalina Domènech Ferrès, second wife of Dalí's father, Salvador Dalí y Cusí. Dalí's mother had died in 1921, and his father married his late wife's sister in 1924. Fèlix Fanés (211) wonders what effect such "incest" must have had on Dalí.

landscape... like a huge aqueduct: A similar image occurs in the "Ode to Salvador Dalí": "The air polishes its prism over the sea / and the horizon rises like a great aqueduct."

coral... Virgin holds: A statue of the Virgin in which Lorca had placed a piece of coral (Gibson, *FGL1,* 405, 411).

ballerinas of glass: probably, the bead curtains which hung in the doorway to prevent flies from entering.

crespell: A sweet Catalan pastry, baked in the shape of a star, and eaten on Easter.

Lidia: Lidia Noguer i Sabà (1886-1946), fishwife of Cadaqués, was so obsessed with the Catalan writer Eugenio D'Ors that she came to believe she was Teresa, protagonist of D'Ors's philosophical novel *La ben plantada* (1912) (RST, *SD escribe,* 123 and ff.; Sánchez Vidal 114-115). To her, Dalí dedicated his essay "St. Sebastian." Later, Noguer served as inspiration for the character "Teresa la Ben Plantada" in D'Ors's *The True History of Lidia de Cadaqués* (1954, with illustrations by Dalí). See also Cristina Masanés, *Lidia de Cadaqués: Crbnica d'un deliri* (Barcelona: Quaderns Crema, 2001). A few years later, D'Ors was to write an article harshly critical of Dalí in *La Gaceta Literaria* (Dec. 15, 1929), mentioning a recently exhibited picture on which the painter had written "I spit on the portrait of my mother." When the news reached Dalí's father, he severed relations with his son (Fanés, 198).

188 ***two brave fishermen:*** Lidia's two sons, Filemón and Bancis (Gibson, *FGL1*, 411), one of whom, like Lidia herself, died in an insane asylum.

Anna Maric: "He liked to call me Anna *Maric*" (letter of June 17, 1981 from Anna María Dalí to C. Maurer)

Puig Pujades: Lorca alludes to the portly Catalan Josep Puig Pujades (1882-1940)—tailor, journalist, novelist and politician—whom he had met during his stay in Cadaqués. Dalí illustrated his novel *L'oncle Vicenç* (1926). (*Dalí et les livres*, 87)

mona: Anna María Dalí's godfather had given her a traditional Catalan pastry called *mona*, which she had shared with her family and Federico.

Nublo: Amused by the Catalan word "núvol," Lorca had asked Anna María "how do you say *nublo* (cloud)?"

Notary: Dalí's father was a notary public.

2.

drawing of white mantilla: It is uncertain to which drawing Dalí is referring, though it would certainly have resembled "Mantilla of Madroños" (which seems to have formed part of a 1925 letter to Anna María Dalí) and "Lady on Balcony with a Mantilla of Madroños" (*See* Hernández, nos. 73 and 74).

3.

Cézanne's grand ambition: In 1904 Cézanne declared that he wanted "to do Poussin again, [this time] after nature" and to make Impressionism "something solid and durable like the Old Masters."

Guillermo de Torre (1900-1971), avant-garde poet and literary critic, brother in law of Jorge Luis Borges.

Halffter: Ernesto Halffter (1905-1989), a disciple of Lorca's friend Manuel de Falla.

5.

Iron butterfly: It is unknown what Lorca text—letter? poem? essay?—Dalí is referring to.

Polyclete. According to the *Columbia Encyclopedia,* the "'canon of Polykleitos,' which emphasized a counterbalance of tension and relaxation through shoulders and hips, known as chiastic balance, became the standard of proportions for sculptors. It is best known through a copy, the *Doryphorus* or *Spear-Bearer* (Naples)."

La Bien Plantada: "fine-looking", attractive, resourceful, self-confident woman: sobriquet of Lidia of Cadaqués.

constructing the void; plasticity of hollows: Lorca would attempt to do the same, years later, in *Poet in New York,* where the *vacío* and the *hueco* are key images.

6.

Grosz, Pascin: The German Georg Grosz (1893-1959) and the Bulgarian-French painter Jules Pascin (1885-1930) published their satirical works in *Simplicissimus* and other German magazines.

sketch putrefaction: In a letter from Figueras to Pepín Bello of Dec. 18, 1925, Dalí comes as close as he ever did to defining putrefaction: "In a little while I'm going to publish a book of my putrifieds with a preface by Federico. In the last analysis, putrefaction is SENTIMENT. Therefore it is something inseparable from human nature. As long as there is an atmosphere around the earth, there is putrefaction. The only thing outside our atmosphere is astronomy, and that is why we oppose astronomy to Putrefaction... In the little book, in order to disinfect it from so much putrefaction, I will include six invitations to astronomy (sketches in a certain style invented by me)" (*SD escribe,* 122; Sánchez Vidal 153). Finkelstein writes that in Dalí's writing of this period, the appellation *putrefactos* "designates philistines and conformists, especially in the arts. The poet Rafael Alberti recalled that "putrefacto"" constituted a kind of summing up of all that was decrepit, dead and anachronistic in various people and objects... The term eventually was used to refer to everything: literature, painting, style of dress, houses, the most disparate objects and anything that smelled rotten or might hinder or prevent unobstructed progress" (Finkelstein, *Dalí's Art and Writing,* 31). Another companion from the Residencia, the painter José Moreno Villa, wrote that *putrefacto* implied "a mind that is punctilious and peevish, hollow, full of commonplaces, of routine and idiotic prudence. [...] [Sometimes it was a question of] appearance. The painter Dalí designed a whole book, and I saw drawings in which the 'putrefact' was really disgusting. Apparently his most characteristic feature was his moustache..." (Ades 139).

7.

Exhibition: An exhibition of 22 works (seventeen paintings and five drawings) at the Dalmau Gallery, Barcelona, November 14-27, 1925. One of the paintings exhibited was *Syphon and Bottle of Rum,* which Lorca gave to Lorca (now in the Museo Nacional Reina Sofía, Madrid).

"harshest criticism" of exhibition: Finkelstein quotes from the clipping: "The critic acknowledged that Dalí's temperament was receptive to any attempt at innovation. Dalí, he wrote, discards past styles "since his intelligence, illuminated by his profound knowledge of painting, has shown him that these are of no help in attaining the one and only proposed ideal: lyricism. Thus we find in Salvador Dalí one of the most qualified and capable representatives of Cubism and schools derived from it" (Finkelstein, *Dalí's Art and Writing,* 17).

Barradas: The Uruguayan painter Rafael Barradas (1890-1929), a close friend of both Lorca and Dalí, who led a lively weekly gathering of artists and writers in the Barcelona suburb of Hospitalet. In 1921 he had designed the stage sets for Lorca's first play.

8.

Cap de Creus. Rocky point with beaches (now a national park) a little north of Cadaqués, shown in many paintings by Dalí, where the "Tramontana" wind has carved the rocks into fantastical shapes (for example, the "orange-colored eagle" mentioned in this letter). Photos in Gibson, *Shameful Life*, 69-71.

Casa Pichot: The house of the family of Ramón Pichot (also spelled Pitxot) Gironés and Antonia Gironés, family friends of the Dalís. Various members of the family were artists: the cellist Ricard (captured by Dalí in a 1920 portrait; *D* 66), the violinist Lluís, the opera singer María (whose nickname was Niní), and a second sister, Mercedes, who was married to one of Lorca's mentors in his first days in Madrid: the playwright Eduardo Marquina (Fanés, 223).

Iphigenia: This work, never found and perhaps never written, was inspired by a visit to the ruins of the port of Empúries, where FGL looked at an ancient mural portraying the sacrifice of Iphigenia, daughter of Agamemnon and Clytemestra (Gibson, *FGL1*, 405).

Xenius: Pen name of Eugenio D'Ors, whose influence made itself felt in Dalí's theory of "Holy Objectivity."

rrrare folks: FGL rolls his r's, imitating a postcard Lidia had sent to Eugenio D'Ors on March 14, 1925—a postcard Anna María probably intercepted and sent to Federico.

Halffter: The composer Ernesto Halffter was a friend both of Lorca and of Dalí, who sent him a drawing for the cover of his *Marche joyeuse* in 1925.

Visca!: Long live Catalonia!

portrait: The portrait in question, entitled *Slavdor Adil,* was included with this letter. A dedication, crossed out, reads, "For my friend Anna María Dalí. Portrait of her brother." (*See* Color Illustrations)

9.

Project of the waves: Probable allusion to Lorca's poem "The Siren and the Carabineer" (CP 759-60), of which he speaks in a letter to Jorge Guillén on March 2, 1926: "A flat light, and *love and serenity* in the form. It will be a *huge bore,* but I am profoundly moved by this story. It is the myth of the useless beauty of the sea. [...] I would like the water to grow calm, so I can meticulously describe one wave (the first) and then a second one, and then the third, until we come upon a little boat..." (CP, 857). For the image of "counting the waves," see the introduction, and Dalí's comment in his essay "Saint Sebastian."

BOOBY: "ñañes" in the original: from the Catalan nyanyes or *nyanyo,* which can mean a swelling caused by a bruise or the sores caused by syphilis (RST, *SD escribe,* 122).

St. Vicens: An allusion to a friend from the Residencia, Juan Vicens (1985-1958).

Mister Carter: The archaeologist Howard Carter (1873-1939), discoverer of the tomb of Tutankhamen, had lectured at the Residencia de Estudiantes.

Natalie: The actress Natalie Talmadge, whom Buster Keaton married in 1921.

10.

Joan of Arc: the saint had just been named patron of wireless telegraphy because of the voices she heard as a child (RST, *SD escribe,* 121).

postcards from Paris: The friends sending Dalí postcards from the "Select American Bar" (mentioned in Hemingway's *The Sun Also Rises*) are Juan Vicéns (1885-1958), the poet José María Hinojosa (1904-1906), Luis Buñuel (1900-1983), and the writer and painter José Moreno Villa (1887-1955). The letter may be slightly earlier: Hinojosa's unpublished correspondence in the archives of the Residencia de Estudiantes shows that he arrived in Paris in July and and left for London in September 1925.

Buster Keaton: Reference to *The Navigator.*

Cover for Songs: Lorca did not use this cover—if it was ever sent to him—when *Canciones* was published in 1927.

bookplate: the bookplate of a bullfighter and bull is reproduced in *SD escribe,* 18.

"Long live the rose on its bush": Dalí quotes from Lorca's poem "Encuentro" (Encounter) in the suite "El jardín de las morenas" (Garden of the Brownhaired Girls), *CP* 180.

11.

Cocteau: Dalí is quoting from "Tour du secteur calme" published in

Poésie (1916-1923), Paris, Gallimard, 1925, 2-6 (RST, *SD escribe*, 126-27).

"Saturday, garden gate": From Lorca's "Schoolboy's Song," *Songs* (CP 417), which Dalí saw in manuscript.

Book about putrefaction. The book was to have included satirical sketches by Dalí and a prologue by Lorca, but the poet never provided it. Sketches probably intended for the book were collected by Santos Torroella in 1995.

"Buster Keaton's Stroll": a dramatic dialogue ("Paseo de Buster Keaton") Lorca had written in 1925. For an English translation, see García Lorca, *Barbarous Nights: Legends and Plays from The Little Theater*, tr. Christopher Sawyer-Lauçanno (San Francisco: City Lights Books, 1991), 61-65.

Photo with Lidia: see black and white illustrations.

Photo of painting: RST (126) identifies the painting with *Venus y Cupidillos* (also known as *Venus and Amorini*) (*D* 212).

12.

Covers for magazine: Dalí has been invited to submit a cover for *gallo*, the literary magazine Lorca and his friends were to publish in Granada in 1928.

Girl in Figueras: Finkelstein believes Dalí is referring to "Young Girl in Figueres (thus named in the catalogue of the second Dalmau exhibition; also known as *Woman at the Window in Figueres*" (*Dalí's Art and Writing*, 20). The reference might also be to "Girl from the Back" (*D* 231).

Margarita: Margarita Manso, who had studied previously with Dalí at the School of Fine Arts. Lorca dedicates one of his *Gypsy Ballads* to her. See also Gibson, *Shameful Life*, 178-81: Dalí recalls that, wanting to sleep with *him* and unable to, Lorca satisfied his desire by attempting to possess Manso.

Daddy Lebonnard: Allusion to *Le Père Lebonnard,* a play by Jean Aicard (1890).

Antonio Moreno. The actor bore a strange similarity to the writer—a mentor and mutual friend of Lorca and Dalí—José Moreno Villa (RST, *SD escribe,* 127)

Fortuny: The painter and designer Mariano Fortuny y Madrazo (1871-1949), an influence on Dalí's later work.

13.

Salisacs: Reference to Pere Salisacs, a rich merchant of Cadaqués, who had a house near that of the Dalí family. According to Anna María Dalí, Pedrito Salisacs (Pere's oldest son) taught her and Dalí to dance the Charleston in the summer of 1926, using records he brought back from London (*SD* escribe 129 and Rodrigo 90-91).

15.

Señoritas of Granada: See "Preface," above, p. 25.

Beasts: Allusion to an association founded by the painter Santiago Rusiñól, "Noah's Ark," whose members took animal names (Rodrigo 197, n. 25).

16.

Between this letter and the preceding one, Dalí had been expelled from the Special School of Painting, Madrid, after having declared that the board was not competent to examine him.

Painting waves: Dalí might be referring to *Rocks at Llané* (D 244). Dawn Ades (136) remarks: "It comes as no surprise that [Dalí's] next favorite painter beside Vermeer was the *Douanier* Rousseau, whose idea of realism was to paint every individual leaf on a tree."

Pani: hill overlooking Cadaqués. See Dalí's *View of Cadaqués from Mount Pani* (D 93).

exams: In September 1926, Lorca had written to various friends confessing his anguish over having no career but poetry and declaring that, in order to please his parents, he had decided to prepare himself for examinations leading to a professorship. See, for example, the letter to Jorge Guillén (*SL*, 82).

Brussels: Dalí had made a first trip to Brussels and Paris (where he met Picasso) in April 1926, in the company of his sister and aunt.

Exhibition: Dalí's second one-man exhibition was at the Dalmau Galleries, Barcelona, from Dec. 31, 1926 to Jan. 14, 1927.

rocks, my breadbaskets, my girls sewing: Allusions to *Anna María, Sewing* (D 230); *Woman at the Window at Figueras* (D 239); *Rocks at Llané* (D 244 and 245), *Penya-Segats (Woman on the Rocks)* (D 246); and *Basket of Bread* (D 249).

17.

drawings for my books: Lorca was planning to publish at *Litoral*, Málaga, "Ode to Salvador Dalí," *Gypsy Ballads, Songs, Suites*, and *Poem of the Deep Song*.

brother in Paris: Francisco García Lorca (1902-1976) who was studying in France, preparing himself for a career in the foreign service.

dedicated poem: "Tree of Song" in *Songs* (CP 467)

18.

flounder: "...a reference, perhaps, to the somewhat ambiguous sexual connotation of the fish as a representation of both male and female genitalia" (Finkelstein, *Dalí's Art and Writing*, 25-26).

anti-elegance, convalescence: St. Sebastian was nursed back to life by St. Irene after surviving the onslaught of the Emperor's arrows.

Blessed Rigol: the painter Josep Rigol i Fornaguera (1897-1986), who had studied with Dalí at the Escuela de San Fernando, Madrid (RST, *SD escribe*, 133). See Dalí's drawing, "Portrait of Rigol" (1924) in *Dalí residente*, 145.

Litoral: the literary magazine run by poets Emilio Prados and Manuel Altolaguirre in Málaga, where Lorca published some of his *Gypsy Ballads*.

Maroto: The painter and writer Gabriel García Maroto, who had published Lorca's *Book of Poems* in 1921. The portrait, now in the Museo Nacional de Artes Plásticas, Montevideo, is reproduced in *EY*, 30.

19.

El Gallo del Defensor: An early title for the literary magazine *gallo*, which was to be published as a supplement to a Granada newspaper.

soldier: Dalí did his military service in the Castillo de San Fernando,

Figueras, within sight of his house, where he slept at night (RST, *SD escribe*, 170).

"my St. Sebastian" (141-150), article dedicated to Lorca and published in the July 31, 1927 issue of *L'Amic de les Arts*.

Mantegna... irony?! See Dalí's essay, "St. Sebastian," which is adumbrated here. Santos Torroella (*SD escribe*) points out that Dalí would probably have seen Mantegna's *Saint Sebastian* in the Louvre in 1926.

20.

Lorca's historical drama *Mariana Pineda* opened on June 24 in Barcelona, with stage sets by Dalí. The best edition is *Mariana Pineda,* translated with an introduction and commentary by Robert G. Havard (Warminster/Wiltshire: Aris and Philips, 1987).

21.

Dipping peseta notes: "I shall only tell you that one of my favorite gems at this time was to dip bank notes into my whiskey until they began to disintegrate. This involved a long ceremonial which would dumbfound those who happened to witness it. I loved to practice this trick while I argued, with a refined avarice, about the price of one of those modest *demi-mondaines* who offer themselves to you body and soul, saying 'Give me whatever you like!'" *The Secret Life of Salvador Dalí,* 203).

my poem: Dalí sent Lorca copies of several prose poems, but it is uncertain which one he is referring to here.

22.

Songs. Lorca's second book of poems, *Songs 1921-1924,* had been published by *Litoral,* Málaga, in May 1927 (*See* CP 442-543)

Orange and lemon: There is an English translation in CP, 494-96.

23.

Written after Lorca's second visit to Cadaqués in summer 1927; dense with private allusion.

Qucurucuchs: Local name for two islands in the bay of Cadaqués (RST, *Dalí residente,* 177).

where Venus was born: Dalí had already painted *Venus and Amorini* (D 212) and several versions of *Venus and Sailor* (D 220-222, 224).

Apparatuses, woman cut to pieces: Allusion to *Honey is Sweeter than Blood,* which Dalí was painting when Lorca was in Cadaqués (*D* 262) and which bore the preliminary title *El bosc d'aparells* (The Forest of Apparatuses). The title was suggested by Lidia Noguer, who compared Eugenio D'Ors to her own sons with the words: "honey is sweeter than blood!" The severed torso of a woman (and pool of blood) also appears in *Cenicitas.* On Dalí's image of the "apparatus" or "gadget," see Finkelstein, *Dalí's Art and Writing,* 53-54.

Salleras: a neighbor of the Dalí family on the beach of Llané (RST, *Dalí residente,* 178). The "sardana" (Catalan regional dance) mentioned does not seem to exist, but the title reminded RST of another sardana: "Per tu ploro" (RST, *Dalí residente,* 178).

Raimunda: friend of the Dalí family.

"Paint my name into the picture": Little Cinders: Cenicitas, first known as *The Birth of Venus* and later named by Lorca *Els esforços estèrils* (Sterile Efforts), (1927-1928), (*D* 265; *400 Obres I, no. 122*) depicts the severed head of Lorca, half buried in the sand, alongside the "yellow measuring stick" mentioned in the "Ode."

Article about my exhibition: Lorca had exhibited his drawings at the Dalmau Galleries in June 1927, and Dalí reviewed them in "Federico García Lorca: Exposició de dibuixos colorits," *La Nova Revista* (Barcelona) 3 (9) (September 1927), 84-85. There is an English translation and commentary by Finkelstein in *Collected Writings,* 49, 50 and 39. See notes to letter 24.

24.

Dalmau: Josep Dalmau i Rafel (1867-1937), painter, merchant, and restorer of pictures, who ran an art gallery on the Passeig de Gràcia, Barcelona from 1923 to 1930 (Anderson, *Epistolario,* 502).

Sucre: The writer and critic José María de Sucre y de Grau (1886-1969) (Anderson, *EC,* 502).

Picabia: The French painter was a friend of Dalmau, and had exhibited his watercolors at his gallery in 1922. See Agnes de la Beaumelle, *La Revue du Louvre et des Musées de France,* 50:1 (Feb. 2000): 65-7, 116.

"Drop of Water": In a review of Lorca's Dalmau exhibition Dalí writes, a propos of this drawing (now lost): "One of Lorca's best sketches, the "Drop of Water," for example, seems infiltrated by the purest, most

exquisite oriental poisons: those subtle, deadly poisons that, just when the anemia of the plastic arts of the West is at the highest, most dangerous point, have often been transformed into an elixir of longevity and rejuvenation." He adds: "The plastic creation of Lorca flows at times, and in its finest moments, from the graphic life of various lines dictated by the Surrealists, as well as by the silly iridescent decorativeness of the spirals in the innards of crystal balls. // This aphrodisiac and poetic figuration of the recently exhibited drawings by Lorca holds for us, however, a single flaw, a flaw probably never to be associated with the people of Ampurdan: the increasingly irresistible flaw of exquisiteness brought to the extreme" (tr. Finkelstein, *Collected Writings*, 48-49).

I'm sending you these drawings: The drawings have not been preserved.

25.

St. Sebastian.... not lashed to a gnarled tree trunk: For Renaissance renderings, see Darriulat and the "Iconography of St. Sebastian" at http: //bode.diee.unica.it/~giua/SEBASTIAN/. It was, in fact, during the Middle Ages that St. Sebastian was first shown lashed to a tree-trunk, and during the Renaissance that he was depicted tied to a marble column. See the sources cited by Moinet, 20.

breeze from the sea: Lorca was vacationing with his family at a spa in Lanjarón, south of Granada.

The end of this letter is lost.

26.

My dear little pictures: RST (*SD escribe,* 138) points out that Dalí was about to exhibit in Barcelona (in the "Salón de Otoño", Sala Parés) *Apparatus and Hand* (*D* 264) and *Honey is Sweeter Than Blood* (*D* 262)

27.

Miró: the Catalan painter, who exhibited his work at the Dalmau gallery between 1918 and 1923, visited Dalí in Figueras in September 1927 and wrote to him praising his work that December (the letter is reproduced in *DJ*, 33). See Dalí's essay of 1928 in *Collected Writings*, 93-94 and *EY*, 224; and Rafael Santos Torroella, "Unas cartas de Miró a Dalmau", *Kalías* 5:9 (1993): 64-77.

Juan Ramón: A while earlier, in summer 1925, Dalí had sent the poet Juan Ramón Jiménez two drawings—female nudes—which JRJ published in his plaquette *Ley* (RST, *SD escribe,* 94-97). They became antagonists when Dalí and Buñuel sent JRJ an insulting letter about his famous novella of a boy and his donkey, *Platero y yo:* "Sr. Dn. Juan Ramón Jiménez / Madrid. / Our distinguished friend: We believe it is our duty to tell you—disinterestedly—that we find your work profoundly repugnant—it is hysterical, cadaverous, immoral and arbitrary.// Especially: // MERDE!!! // for your *Platero and I,* for your facile and badly intentioned *Platero and I,* the *least* donkey-like donkey, the most odious donkey we have ever run into. // And for you, too, on account of your creepy behavior: // MIERDA!! // Sincerely, // Luis Buñuel, Salvador Dalí" (Sánchez Vidal, 189).

Benjamín Palencia: painter from La Mancha (1894-1980), a friend of Lorca and an admirer of Juan Ramón Jiménez.

"Poem of the Little Things": For other versions of this poem, see the one published in *L'Amic de les Arts* (Sitges), 27, Aug. 31, 1928 (*EY* 224) and the version sent to Pepín Bello (Sánchez Vidal, 164).

28.

Prados, Altolaguirres: The poets Emilio Prados (1899-1962) and Manuel Altolaguirre (1905-1959), who ran the small press, *Litoral,* where Lorca published *Songs. Verso y Prosa* was a literary magazine from Murcia.

great vulgar pig Rubén Darío: The playwright Ramón del Valle-Inclán had famously described the modernist poet as a "cerdo triste" (sad pig).

Casa Colom: an example of *art nouveau* architecture which Dalí later came to admire.

Muñozes, Porredones, Calandres: I am uncertain to whom Dalí is alluding.

29.

my "poem" with photographs for gallo: It is unknown what poem Dalí is referring to; perhaps "Peix perseguit per un raïm" (Fish Pursued by a Bunch of Grapes), which was published not in *gallo* but in *L'Amic de les Arts* (Sitges) 3.28 (September 31, 1928): 217-18 and *L'Amic de les Arts* 4 (31) (March 31, 1929): 9. For another translation, see Finkelstein, *Collected Writings*, 28-30.

30.

very beautiful smiling woman: It is not clear which painting Dalí is referring to. Similar motifs appear in *Little Cinders.*

stray breasts: See Dalí's essay "...The Liberation of the Fingers...," in *Collected Writings,* 99-101 and *Salvador Dalí: The Early Works,* 229.

Rotting donkey: Possibly, Dalí's *L'ase podrit* (also known as *The Donkey's Carcass*), finished in 1928. Cf. the famous scene from *Un chien andalou.* In "The Liberation of the Fingers" (published in March 1929), Dalí writes that "in 1927, three of us, without the slightest contact, and distant from each other for a long time, coincidentally came across the rotting donkey: I was then at Cadaqués, carrying out a series of paintings, in which there appeared as an obsessive theme a kind of rotting donkey full of flies; I received two letters, almost simultaneously: one from Pepín Bello, from Madrid, in which he spoke to me of the rotting donkey and described things with a total resemblance in details to other things I had recently written; a few days later, Luis Buñuel spoke to me of a rotting donkey in a letter from Paris" (Raeburn, *EY,* 228).

Fontanals or Alarma: Manuel Fontanals (1893-1972), who later worked with Lorca on the Buenos Aires production of *La zapatera prodigiosa* (The Shoemaker's Prodigious Wife) and Salvador Alarma i Tastàs (1870-1941) (RST, *SD escribe,* 142).

Anti-Artistic magazine: Dalí never founded a literary magazine, but in his "Yellow Manifesto (Catalan Antiartistic Manifesto)" in *Collected Writings,* 59-63, where he denounces "the unhealthy sentimentality dished up by the Orfeó Català with its worn-out repertoire of popular songs adapted and adulterated by people who are absolutely hopeless in what concerns music..." See also *Salvador Dalí: The Early Years*, 221-222.

32.

Enriquet: Enrique Giró, a fisherman whom Dalí used to hire as a sailor during his trips to Cadaqués (RST, *SD escribe*, 140).

Souday: The book is *Paul Valéry*, Paris, Kra, 1927.

Si le grain ne meurt: Gide's autobiography, published in Éditions de la NRF in 1924.

Gómez de la Serna: The Spanish writer and man of letters (1888-1963), known for his lyrical aphorisms, was a friend of Lorca during his early days in Madrid, and his style influences that of the poet in "St. Lucy and St. Lazarus" and in other works of the 1920s. Gómez de la Serna would later write a book on Dalí. See C. Maurer, "García Lorca y el Ramonismo." *Boletín de la Fundación Federico García Lorca*, III, no. 5 (1989): 55-60.

photography, film: See Dalí's essays "Photography: Pure Creation of the Spirit," "Art Film, Antiartistic Film," and "The Photographic Donnée" (or "The Photographic Data") in *Collected Writings*, 45-47, 53-57, 68-69 and in *Salvador Dalí: The Early Years*, 216, 219-220, 227.

33.

prodigious poem: Fragment from a lost letter, quoted by Lorca in one of his own letters to Jorge Zalamea: see *EC* 578.

34.

Salvador de Horta (1520-1567) was born in Santa Coloma de Farnés (Gerona) and was a shepherd and shoemaker as a child. After becoming a Franciscan he served in various monasteries and became known for his miracles. Lorca seems to be referring to an image of him.

Dalí's "prodigious poem": "Saint Sebastian," first published in Catalan in *L'Amic de les Arts,* II:16 (July 31, 1927), 52-54, and in Spanish translation in the first issue of Lorca's literary magazine *gallo* (February 1928), 9-12. This was Dalí's first essay for the prestigious arts journal, and the beginning of his public career as writer.

little bear: Lorca is referring to one of Anna María's childhood toys (much talked about during the visit to Cadaqué), a stuffed bear, "Osito," which he renamed "Osito Marquina" because it resembled the playwright Eduardo Marquina. The bear is now in the Museo del Juguete (Toy Museum), Figueras. See Carmen Torres Ripa, "El 'Museo del juegete' en Figueras, es un recinto para el recuerdo...", *El Correo Español* (Bilbao), 10 Sept. 1989.

36.

This letter served as rough draft for Dalí's important article "Reality and Surreality" (translation in *Collected Writings,* 94-99 and *Salvador Dalí: The Early Years,* 225-26), published in *La Gaceta Literaria* 44:15 (Oct. 15, 1928).

Andrenio: pseudonym of the critic Eduardo Gómez de Baquero, who had reviewed *The Gypsy Ballads.*

chunks of incest: Dalí confuses "St. Eulalia" with the ballad "Thamar and Amnon."

carries her down to the river: Allusion to "La casada infiel" (The Faithless Wife).

"You move within accepted anti-poetic notions": In his essay on Joan Miró, published in June 1928, Dalí makes a similar comment: "Indeed, in a particularly casual state of mind, hence free from all imaginative action (which is always contrary to any passive moment), the spectacle of a stationary cart with its awning, hitched up to an animal, can suddenly be converted into the most detailed and disturbing magical whole, once one considers the awning of the cart and the cords moved by the wind as a living and throbbing part of the whole, since really they are the only things moving in front of our eyes and, in contrast, the still horse as an inanimate, inert continuation of the wheels and the wood" (*EY*, 224).

Civil Guard: Cf. "Romance de la guardia civil española" (Ballad of the Civil Guard).

"Let the gentlemen know": From "Muerto de amor" (Dead from Love): "Mother, when I die / I want the gentlemen to know. / Send blue telegrams / from South to North" (CP 559.

"Little eyes": From "El emplazado" (Ballad of the Marked Man): "My aloneness with no rest! / The small eyes of my body / and the great ones of my horse" (CP 559)

Nestorian: Allusion to the painter Néstor Martín Fernández de la Torre (1887-1938), whose work was considered "putrefacto" by both Dalí and Lorca.

"sterile effort": the title Lorca had given to one of Dalí's paintings (*See* note to letter 23).

37.

exhibition in New York: Nothing is known about the show Lorca was planning, or about his plans—in 1930—to return to New York..

black poet: It is doubtful whether Lorca ever made a film with a "black poet" (his script *Trip to the Moon* was written in collaboration with the Mexican Emilio Amero), and it is even more doubtful that it was to be premiered at this unidentified cinema.

fraud: While Lorca was in Cuba, in April 1930, Dalí had written to his parents telling him that Lorca owed him money (Anderson in EC 694).

38.

Sacher Massoch: See "Les pantoufles de Picasso" (Picasso's Slippers), published in *Cahiers d'art* (Paris) in 1935, and Finkelstein's commentary in *Collected Writings*, 297-301 and 277-78. On Ludwig II of Bavaria, *Ibid.*, 248

Max Aub: Spanish playwright and writer, (1903-1972).

Oda a Salvador Dalí / Ode to Salvador Dalí

Federico García Lorca

Begun in summer 1925, finished in March 1926, published in *Revista de Occidente* (Madrid) the following month. Lorca refers to this poem in a letter as "Didactic Ode to Salvador Dalí" (*E* 336), a good description of its intent. For an excellent commentary see Soria Olmedo, *Fábula,* 141-50.

The reader should remember that the Dalí of 1925 and early 1926 was at work on more or less "realistic" paintings in the spirit of what he called (borrowing a phrase from the Catalan writer Eugenio D'Ors) "Holy Objectivity": *Basket of Bread, Girl Sewing, Port of Cadaqués,* and the early portraits of his father and sister. To Lorca, his style, like that of Jorge Guillén and of Góngora (the lecture on the great Baroque poet was written around the same time), had come to symbolize an aesthetic of unsentimental clarity. Fèlix Fanés (120) writes perceptively that Lorca is alluding in his "Ode" to two aspects of Dalí's art: "the sensual imaginative universe controlled by the Greco-Latin tradition, which is the world of Cadaqués, and the industrial, urban mechanized world" inspired by the Le Corbusier's Parisian publication *L'Esprit Nouveau.* Santos Torroella (*Dalí, Época de Madrid,* 23) describes the period of Dalí's painting Lorca had known at the Residencia: "diverse impregnations which range from Futurism to Purism and to the Italian Metaphysical painters associated with the magazine *Valori Plastici* (1918-1922), especially influenced by Juan Gris [...], the "Vibrationism" of [Rafael] Barradas and the "Planismo" of Celso Lagar." See also Dawn Ades, "Morphologies of Desire," in *EY,* 129-60. Line 3: For Lorca's negative judgments on Impressionism (*See* "Sketch de la nueva pintura" (A Sketch of the New Painting) 167-182). 6: Manuel de Falla praised Lorca for this image of Cubism, less an allusion to the art of Dalí than to the spirit of modern painting. 27: During his first visit to Dalí, Lorca writes to a friend: "Witches from the Pyrenees come down to beg the sirens for a little light. In this landscape I have heard, for the first time in my life, the true, classic sheperd's flute" (*E* 275). 31: Handkerchiefs of farewell, like the one in "Mariner a terra" (*400 Obres*, I, no. 73)?

Line 39: Cf. Lorca's statement in "Sketch of the New Painting"—"At last the orgy of color has been put to an end." 41: Hygiene—both literally and figuratively, as a defense against the "virus" of sentimentality—was one of Dalí's obsessions in his rebellion against bohemian, neo-Romantic visions of art. His "Antiartistic Manifesto" of 1928 would call for an "estricta asepsia espiritual." 44: See Dalí's comment, above, on painting waves (63). 49 ff: The first draft had read: "The current of time pools and orders itself / in the parallelograms dreamt by the centuries ... / / You are afraid of flowers and the water of the river, / because they are fleeting and they pass like the breeze. / You love definite, exact matter, / indifferent to mysteries and deathly to the worm. / / (Your palette, timid as a foolish bird / pulses in your hands with the seven colors)."

Line 93: Crossed out: "adorned with straight lines and without a single wound." The playing cards suggest harsh light without shadow, as in *The Dispute*. 93: Martín (*Antología* 83) observes that certain figures in the French deck of cards are shown with their hearts exposed and Jessica Cartledge associates this image with the playing cards in Dalí's painting "Pierrot Playing the Guitar" (1925) in *D* 217. 98-101: Lorca censored himself in line 103; the first draft read: "el culo [the behind] of Teresa," alluding, perhaps, to a well-known canvas of Dalí's sister, Anna

María, standing at a window. 105: Crossed out: "our friendship, radiant with heart and with laughter." The line means, literally: "our friendship painted like a game of snakes and ladders." *Oca* is played with dice, and the brightly colored game board shows geese, rivers, etc. 107: An allusion to the Catalan flag. Its four red bars on a field of gold are said to have been traced by the fingers, bloodied in battle, of a Catalan conqueror.

St. Lucy and St. Lazarus

Federico García Lorca

Published in *Revista de Occidente* XVIII:53 (November 1927), 145-155 (the feast days of these two saints are celebrated on December 13 and 17); see Andrew A. Anderson, ed., *Poemas en prosa*. Lorca describes this piece to Sebastià Gasch, the art critic to whom it is dedicated, on August 25, 1927 as follows: "In prose what I am working on now is an essay in which I am most interested. I set for myself two literary themes, I develop them and then I analyze them. And the result is a poem. I try to combine my instinct with the virtuosity that I may possess" (Anderson 2004). Dalí reacted enthusiastically, writing to Gasch: "It seems—oh paradox!—that Lorca is beginning to coincide with me on many points. This piece of writing is very eloquent. Do you remember what I told you, some time ago, about the surface of things? // And yet Lorca is now going through an intellectual phase (*momento*) which I believe will last little (although, given its appearance, *putrified people* will think this is a piece of Surrealist writing" (Gibson 1999, 198-199). Lorca's source for the lives of both St. Lucy and St. Lazarus—as well as that of St.

Sebastian—was *The Golden Legend* of Jacobus de Voragine. Thanks to the popular etymology of her name (from *lux*), St. Lucy is associated with light and is prayed to by those with vision problems. She is often represented in painting with her eyes in her hand or on a salver. Terence McMullen shows that, on Lorca's visits to Barcelona in 1925 and 1927 he was aware of a St. Lucy cult centered on a chapel in the cathedral of Barcelona (many details of which correspond to the cathedral described in the "essay").

St. Raymond Nonnatus: thirteenth century Mercedarian friar to whom a chapel is dedicated in the Barcelona cathedral. According to McMullen, "Lorca is mistaken in crediting Saint Raymond Nonnatus with the legendary voyage in question. It belongs, rather to another contemporary Catalan cleric who was a co-founder of the Mercedarian order, namely Saint Raymond of Peñafort (c. 1175-1275)".

Lepanto: a crucifix carried by Don Juan de Austria in his famous battle against the Turks (1571) is still venerated in the cathedral of Barcelona (McMullen, 12).

St. Sebastian
Salvador Dalí

For an excellent commentary, see Finkelstein, *Salvador Dalí's Art,* p. 24 ff. and *Collected Writings,* 14-16 and 379 ff. See also Gaillemin, 64-78.

Imagination, Inspiration, Evasion

Federico García Lorca

Lecture given 1928-1930 in Granada, Madrid, New York and Havana. The version given at Columbia University on Feb. 10, 1930 was titled "Tres modos de poesía" (Three Modes of Poetry), and the one read in Cuba in Spring 1930 was called "Mecánica de la poesía" (The Mechanics of Poetry). The manuscript has been lost, and I have combined several accounts given in newspapers of the period (for sources, see *Conferencias*, ed. C. Maurer, II, 13-31). It is not always clear whether the reporter is quoting García Lorca from notes taken in shorthand, or simply paraphrasing him. An ellipse (....) indicates a break in the text or a rearrangement on my part.

poetic fact: Anderson (2004) points out that Lorca must have borrowed from Dalí the expression "hecho poético": "As for the 'hecho poético', Dalí writes of 'Sant Sebastià' that '*free and clear of symbolisms, he was a* fact *in his sole and simple presence*', he places a quotation from Le Corbusier concerning the 'fait poétique' as an epigraph to an article published March 1928, and the Catalan phrase 'fet poètic' appears in two articles that he published in September and October 1927."

Green I want you green. The journalist is mistaken: Lorca was referring to his "Romance sonámbulo" (Sleepwalking Ballad) from the same collection.

Sketch of the New Painting

Federico García Lorca

Slide-talk given in the Ateneo of Granada at a session celebrating Lorca's literary magazine *gallo*, Oct. 27, 1928.

Cézanne. The anecdote is told by Ambroise Vollard in *Paul Cézanne: His Life and Art* (New York: Frank-Maurice, Inc., 1926), p. 121: When Vollard was unable to sit still for his portrait by Cézanne the painter exclaimed: "You wretch! You've spoiled the pose. Do I have to tell you again you must sit like an apple? Does an apple move?"

first Cubist painting... 1909: Picasso's *Les Demoiselles d'Avignon,* painted in 1907 (the date of the first Cubist exhibition in Paris) was first exhibited in 1916.

Juan Gris's lecture at the Michelet Amphitheatre at the Sorbonne in May 1924 on "The Possibilities of Painting" had been published in Spanish in the September 1924 issue of *Alfar*. In it, Gris remarks: "Celui qui en peignant une bouteille pense à exprimir sa matière au lieu de peindre un ensemble de formes colorées, mérite d'être verrier plutôt que peintre" See Emmanuel Bréon, *Juan Gris a Boulogne* (Paris: Editions Herschedr, 1992), 80.

Verists: see Dalí's comments on G. Grosz in letter 6, above.

And then we get to 1926: Lorca is probably referring to Breton's *First Manifesto* of 1924.

PROUN: The Russian painter and designer El Lissitsky called "proun" the space where two-dimensional painting intersects with three-dimensional architecture.

Cocteau: In *Le mystère laïc* (Paris: Éditions des Quatre Chemins, 1928), 80, Cocteau writes "Chirico, ou le lieu du crime. // Chirico, cést aussi l'heure du train."

Great painter from Granada: According to Mario Hernández, Lorca is referring to José María Rodríguez Acosta.

Works Cited

Ades, Dawn. "Morphologies of Desire." In Raeburn, ed., *Salvador Dalí: The Early Years*. 129-60.

__________. *Dalí*. London: Thames and Hudson, 1982.

Anderson, Andrew A. "Lorca at the Crossroads: 'Imaginación, inspiración, evasión' and the 'novísimas estéticas'." *Anales de la Literatura Española Contemporánea*, XVI (1991), 149-173.

__________. "García Lorca's *Poemas en prosa* and *Poeta en Nueva York*: Dalí, Gasch, Surrealism, and the Avant-Garde." in Robert G. Havard, *Companion to Spanish Surrealism*, ed. Robert G. Havard (London: Boydell and Brower/Tamesis, 2004), in press.

Bosquet, Alain. *Entretiens avec Salvador Dalí*. Monaco: Édtions du Rocher, 2000.

Dalí, Salvador. *Salvador Dalí rétrospective, 1920-1980*. 2nd ed. Paris: Centre Georges Pompidou, 1980.

__________. *400 obres de 1914 a 1983*. Barcelona: Generalitat de Catalunya / Ministerio de Cultura / Obra Cultural de la Caixa de Pensions, 1983. 2 vols.

_______. *Salvador Dalí escribe a Federico García Lorca [1925-1936]*. Ed. Rafael Santos Torroella. *Poesía. Revista Ilustrada de Información Poética*, nos. 27-28 (1987) (= *SD escribe*)

_______. *Salvador Dalí, Federico García Lorca. Correspondance 1925-1936*. Notes et chronologie de Rafael Santos Torroella. Traduction et adaptation de Sylvie Ponce et Felipe Navarro. Paris: Carrere Editions/E. Simion, 1987.

_______. *Un diari: 1919-1920. Les meves impressions i records íntims*. Ed. Fèlix Fanés. Barcelona: Fundació Gala—Salvador Dalí/ edicions 62, 1994.

_______. *L'alliberament dels dits: Obra catalana completa*. Ed. Fèlix Fanés. Barcelona: Quaderns Crema, 1995.

_______. *The Collected Writings*. Edited and translated by Haim Finkelstein. Cambridge: Cambridge University Press, 1998.

Damase, Jacques, ed. *Saint Sébastien dans l'histoire de l'art despuis le XV siècle*. Cachan (France), 1979.

Darriulat, Jacques. *Sebastien le Renaissant. Sur le martyre de saint Sébastien dans la deuxième moitié du Quattrocento*. Iconographie Isabelle D'Hauteville. Paris: Édtions de la Lagune, 1998.

Descharnes, Robert and Gilles Néret. *Salvador Dalí 1904-1989. The Paintings. Part I, 1904-1946*. Cologne: Taschen, 1993 (=D)

Fanés, Fèlix. "Dalí, García Lorca i la pintura". In Antonio Monegal and José María Micó, eds., *Federico García Lorca i Catalunya*. Barcelona Instituto Universitari de Cultura, Universitat Pompeu Fabra/ Diputació de Barcelona, Area de Cultura, 1998. 117-121.

Finkelstein, Haim. *Salvador Dalí's Art and Writing, 1927-1942. The Metamorphoses of Narcissus*. Cambridge: Cambridge University Press, 1996.

Gaillemin, Jean-Louis. *Salvador Dalí. Désirs inassouvis du purisme au surréalisme 1925-1935*. Paris-New York: Le Passage, 2002.

García Lorca, Federico. *Collected Poems*. Ed. Christopher Maurer. 2nd ed. New York: Farrar, Straus and Giroux, 2001 (= *CP*)

__________. *Deep Song and Other Prose*. Tr. Christopher Maurer. New York: New Directions, 1980 (=*DS*)

__________. *Epistolario completo*. Eds. Andrew A. Anderson and Christopher Maurer. Madrid: Cátedra, 1997 (= *EC*)

__________. *Libro de los dibujos* Ed. Mario Hernández Madrid: Tabapress/ Fundación Federico García Lorca, 1991.

__________. *Obras completas*. Ed. Mìguel García-Posada. 4 vols. Barcelona: Círculo de Lectores/Galaxia Gutenberg, 1996-1997 (= OC)

__________. *Poemas en prosa*. ed. Andrew A. Anderson. Granada: Editorial Comares (Colección La Veleta), 2000.

__________. *Poet in New York*. Ed. Christopher Maurer. 2nd Ed. New York: Noonday Press, 1998.

__________. *A Season in Granada*. Translated and edited by Christopher Maurer. London: Anvil Press Poetry, 1998 (=*SG*)

__________. *Selected Letters*. Tr. David Gershator. New York: New Directions, 1984 (=*SL*)

Gibson, Ian. *Federico García Lorca. I. De Fuente Vaqueros a Nueva York,*

1898-1929. Barcelona: Grijalbo, 1985. (=FGL1)

__________. *Lorca-Dalí. El amor que no pudo ser.* Barcelona: Plaza & Janés, 1999.

__________. *The Shameful Life of Salvador Dalí.* New York: W.W. Norton, 1998.

Hernández, Mario. "García Lorca y Salvador Dalí: Del ruiseñor lírico a los burros podridos (Poética y epistolario)". *L'Imposible/ Posible di Federico García Lorca.* Ed. Laura Dolfi. Naples: Ed. Scientifiche Italiana, 1989. 267-319.

Ilie, Paul. *Documents of the Spanish Vanguard.* Chapel Hill, North Carolina: The University of North Carolina Press, 1969.

Kaye, Richard A. "'Determined Raptures': St. Sebastian and the Victorian Discourse of Decadence." *Victorian Literature and Culture* (1999): 269-303.

McMullen, Terence. "Federico García Lorca's *Santa Lucía y San Lázaro* and the Aesthetics of Transition." *Bulletin of Hispanic Studies,* LXVII (1990), 1-20.

Moinet, Eric. "Hagiographie de *Saint Sébastien.*" in *Le Saint Sébastien soigné par Irène de Georges de La Tour.* Orléans: Ville d'Orléans, 1998.

Monegal, Antonio. "Las palabras y las cosas, según Salvador Dalí." *El aeroplano y la estrella: El movimiento de vanguardia en los Países Catalanes (1904-1936).* Ed. Joan Ramon Resina. Amsterdam/ Atlanta: Rodopi, 1997: 151-76.

Raeburn, Michael. *Salvador Dalí: The Early Years.* London: Thames and

Hudson, 1994 (= *EY*)

Reau, Louis. *Iconographie de l'Art Chrétien*. Vol. 3, *Iconographie des Saints*. Paris, 1959: 1190-99.

Ríos-Font, Wadda. *"La poética de Salvador Dalí y la poesía de Federico García Lorca"*. *Plaza* 11 (1986): 48-56.

Rodrigo, Antonina. *García Lorca en Cataluña*. Barcelona: Planeta, 1975.

Sánchez Vidal, Agustín. *Buñuel, Lorca, Dalí: El enigma sin fin*. Barcelona: Planeta, 1988.

Santos Torroella, Rafael. *La miel es más dulce que la sangre. Las épocas lorquiana y freudiana de Salvador Dalí*. Barcelona: Seix Barral, 1984.

__________. *Dalí residente*. Madrid: Publicaciones de la Residencia de Estudiantes/Consejo Superior de Investigaciones Científicas, 1992.

__________. *Dalí. Época de Madrid*. Madrid: Publicaciones de la Residencia de Estudiantes/Consejo Superior de Investigaciones Científicas, 1994.

__________. *"Los putrefactos" de Dalí y Lorca. Historia y antología de un libro que no pudo ser*. Madrid: Publicaciones de la Residencia de Estudiantes / Consejo Superior de Investigaciones Científicas, 1995.

Soria Olmedo, Andres. *Fabula de fuentes: Tradición y vìda literaria en Federico García Lorca*. Madrid: Residencia de Estrudiantes, 2004.

Stainton, Leslie. *Federico García Lorca: A Dream of Life*. New York: Farrar, Straus & Giroux, 2000.

Zupnick, Irving L. *St. Sebastian in Art.* Ph.D. dissertation, Columbia University, 1958.

Abbreviations

CP	Federico García Lorca, *Collected Poems*
D	Robert Descharnes and Gilles Néret, *Salvador Dalí 1904-1989*
DS	Federico García Lorca, *Deep Song and Other Prose*
EC	Federico García Lorca, *Epistolario completo*
EY	Michael Raeburn, ed., *Salvador Dalí: The Early Years*. London
FGL1	Ian Gibson, *Federico García Lorca. I. De Fuente Vaqueros a Nueva York, 1898-1929*
OC	Federico García Lorca, *Obras completas*
SD	Rafael Santos Torroella, ed., *Salvador Dalí escribe a Federico García Lorca*
SG	Federico García Lorca, *A Season in Granada*

Illustrations

(In order of appearance)

Color Gallery

Salvador Dalí, *Cubist Composition. Still Life of a Person Holding a Letter,* Fundació Gala-Salvador Dalí, Figueras.

Salvador Dalí, *Little Ashes (Cenicitas)*, Museo Nacional Centro de Arte Reina Sofía, Madrid.

Salvador Dalí, *Academia neo-cubista (Neo-Cubist Academy)*, Montserrat Abbey.

Alonso Berruguete, *St. Sebastian,* National Museum of Religious Carving, Valladolid.

Federico García Lorca, *San Sebastian,* private collection, Madrid.

Salvador Dalí, *The Marriage of Buster Keaton,* Fundación Federico García Lorca, Madrid.

Salvador Dalí, *Shoe Collage,* Fundación Federico García Lorca, Madrid.

Salvador Dalí, *San Sebastian* (from a letter), Fundación Federico García Lorca, Madrid

Federico García Lorca, *SLAVDOR ADIL / (Peintre),* Casa-Museo Federico García Lorca, Granada.

Federico García Lorca, *PORTRAIT OF / DALI*, Romero Gómez family, Granada.

Federico García Lorca, *Portrait of Dalí*, Fundació Gala-Salvador Dalí, Figueras.

Salvador Dalí, *Honey is Sweeter than Blood*, location unknown. From a photo in the Fundación Federico García Lorca, Madrid.

Federico García Lorca, *Ecce Homo!*, private collection, Madrid.

Black and White Gallery

Federico García Lorca, *Urquinaona!*, Fundación Federico García Lorca, Madrid.

Federico García Lorca in his room at the Residencia, Fundación Federico García Lorca, Madrid.

Salvador Dalí in his studio in Figueres, Fundación Federico García Lorca, Madrid.

"Lidia gives me a fish," Fundación Federico García Lorca, Madrid.

García Lorca and Dalí on the beach at Cadaqués, Fundación Federico García Lorca, Madrid.

Dalí, Lorca and Anna Maria on the terrace at the Dalí family's home, Fundación Federico García Lorca, Madrid.

Federico García Lorca on the terrace at Cadaqués, Fundación Federico García Lorca, Madrid.

García Lorca with Dalí in soldier's uniform, Fundación Federico García Lorca, Madrid.

Federico García Lorca with Luis Buñuel, Fundación Federico García Lorca, Madrid.

Dalí and Lorca at an amusement park, Fundación Federico García Lorca, Madrid.

Index

Z

Swan Isle Press is a not-for-profit literary press dedicated to publishing the works of exceptional writers of poetry, fiction, and nonfiction.

Swan Isle Press
Chicago, 60640-8790
www.swanislepress.com

Sebastian's Arrows

Designed by Edward Hughes

Typeset in Adobe Jenson, Myriad, and Cezanne

Printed on 55# Glatfelter Natural